£35.

Outdoor Development for Managers

For Susan, Jane, Jade and Alex

Since we landed on the island, my lord, it seems to me that Mr Ernest's epigrams have been particularly brilliant . . . But I find – I seem to find it growing wild, my lord, in the woods, that sayings which would be justly admired in England are not much use on an island.

The Admirable Crichton*
J. M. Barrie

*Reprinted by permission of Hodder and Stoughton Limited

Outdoor Development for Managers

John Bank

Gower

Published by
Gower Publishing Company Limited,
Gower House,
Croft Road,
Aldershot,
Hants GU11 3HR,
England

and

Gower Publishing Company,
Old Post Road,
Brookfield,
Vermont 05036,
USA

Reprinted 1989

British Library Cataloguing in Publication Data

Bank, John
  Outdoor development for managers
  1. Personnel management—Bibliography
  I. Title
658.3   HF5549

ISBN 0-566-02440-3

Typeset in Great Britain by Saxon Printing Limited, Derby.
Printed and bound in Great Britain by Billing & Sons Ltd,
Worcester.

CONTENTS

FOREWORD

by Chris Bonington

Adventure has certainly dominated my life and undoubtedly has helped to mould me into the kind of person I now am. I have taken it to extremes, which would have made a conventional career impossible. In fact my last employer, an executive of Van den Berghs (a subsidiary of Unilever), helped to focus my mind when I asked for three months off to go climbing in Patagonia, only six months after becoming a management trainee. He replied to my request by writing, 'Put as plainly as possible, the time has come for you to make up your mind whether you leave mountaineering or Van den Berghs.' I left Van den Berghs.

But in the years that followed I found very quickly that I had chosen an unusual, in some ways unique, career where success demanded the same attributes as those of any successful executive or team member in a company. Once I started to lead expeditions this was even more the case. There are parallels all the way between running a business venture and a mountaineering expedition.

For a start you have to raise the money, work within a budget, at least break even and ideally make a profit. The initial planning and organisation can either give the venture a very real chance of success or, if there are weaknesses, condemn it to almost inevitable failure. Once on the mountain, there is the same need for good leadership and management that is required in any venture.

There will probably always be a debate on the value of outdoor development for managers, but at the very least I am convinced that tasting adventure in even its mildest and most controlled form can act not only as a stimulant and confidence booster but also as a very real piece of therapy through the sheer concentration and surge of adrenalin that clinging to a rock wall or shooting a rapid in a canoe can command. It can also help individuals to understand both more about themselves in an obviously stressful situation and also more about how a group operates, with the direct consequences of either decisions or acts being immediately and at times painfully obvious.

Perhaps, most important of all, it's not only challenging and different, it's also a lot of fun.

PREFACE

'When I doubt myself, I remember the rocks. If I could do that, there is nothing at this company that I can't do.'

A senior manager

'We came home more willing to take risks, more trusting of each other, and more aware of the special abilities of the people we work with.'

A salesman

'When we left the mountain it looked unchanged. No difference. None of us could say the same about each other.'

An executive

'Sure the company benefits. You get something like this from the company . . . . and you feel like giving it back.'

A shopfloor worker

'I felt that by putting us in "real-life" situations (on the rockface) as opposed to classroom simulations, concepts such as direction, leadership, decision making and just plain listening became much more easily understood.'

MBA student

This last quote from a young British manager on an MBA course found an echo among his classmates. The five-day outdoor development module was rated one of the high points of the entire two-year course.

The growing use of the outdoors for management development on both sides of the Atlantic over the last decade is a development that fits the times. As the recession continues, enterprises must be leaner and tougher to survive and their managers will need more positive attitudes and better skills to lead people and work with them in the harsher environment. As radical changes are thrust on companies from all sides, managers need new skills for managing change in uncertainty. The outdoors is being used to 'shape up' managers and help them to sharpen their skills.

Many major companies claim real benefits from using well-conceived outdoor activities for leadership training, team building, improving communication, and speeding up decision making. Individual managers acknowledge these goals but also talk of more individual ones such as overcoming fears, conducting a personal audit of resources, renewing their efforts to stay physically fit, counteracting stress and burn-out.

The file to date on the effective use of the outdoors for management development is fragmented. Most entries come from individuals writing about their experiences in outdoor development or from business journalism full of rich anecdotes of male executives abseiling a rock face or shooting rapids in white-water canoeing. The press conjures up images of company directors and their chief accountants attacking a mountain with the same aggression they use for mergers. The physical side of outdoor activities becomes exaggerated to give outdoor development a 'macho' or an 'officer and a gentleman' image which distorts the entire concept. In the media, outdoor management programmes tend to look like a cheap remake of *Where Eagles Dare* with executives (instead of aging actors) to play the part of young soldiers. Beyond the hype is there a new opportunity for genuine learning and development? Is outdoor development as relevant for women managers as for men?

The full potential of outdoor development courses can only be seen when companies spell out clearly what they want their managers to achieve and when outdoor development organisations meet those objectives with well-designed outdoor activities and systematic debriefings. There is a real need to draw on the experiences of both companies using outdoor development and organisations offering it to examine the criteria to be used in deciding:

1 which sort of outdoor activities are relevant to what management development needs;
2 appropriate objectives for the company, group or individual involved;
3 how courses can develop participants' awareness of managerial/organisational issues and their own managerial skills;
4 How courses can help managers progress from simple problem solving to coping with ambiguity and uncertainty, and with conflicting views on the definition of the problem and on ways of tackling it;
5 the framework within which participants can review their own performance;
6 the acceptability of event design and tutorial resource;
7 the suitability of the particular methods adopted by the organisation offering the activity; and
8 risk-taking activities within a framework of security.

This book is just a beginning. Much work needs to be done on constructing the conceptual framework for outdoor development to show its theoretical underpinnings and its serious learning intent. It is neither a lark, nor is it simply another vogue management technique. The little serious writing published about outdoor development reveals the newness of the topic and the urgent need for greater analysis. A handful of people who write about the topic cannot even agree on what to call it. I have chosen 'outdoor development' because the two words, for me, encapsulate the essence of the process. It is a developmental activity which takes place in an outdoor setting. Others use the phrase 'development training' which leaves out a rather key factor that it takes place out-of-doors. The word 'training' can also imply something that is done to a passive student rather than a bold initiative of experiential learning. Still, many people use the specific name 'outward bound' to refer to the broader field. When they remember to qualify the brand name 'Outward Bound', they end up with a mouthful of words that run on like the name of a Welsh village as in 'an Outward-Bound-kind-of-management-training-programme'. Coupling the word 'adventure' to other words as in 'adventure training' or 'adventure-based management development' adds to the confusion and borders on hyperbole. A solo trek to the North Pole is correctly called an 'adventure', whereas climbing Scafell Pike with a group of managers is not really an adventure. The term 'outdoor management development' seems a little too restrictive as the pedagogy can also be used with non-managers. I hope the people involved will eventually agree on a nomenclature and I'll argue for 'outdoor development.'

GEC, one of Britain's excellent companies, send 2,000 apprentices, trainees, supervisors and managers each year on outdoor development courses. They have been doing so for ten years. Derek Webb, GEC development training advisor, said: 'Probably the most difficult obstacle to surmount, in promoting the concept of outdoor development as a relevant training method, is the ingrained perception of a number of managing directors and personnel directors that outdoor "hairy-chested" training is a "jolly" and that it has no relevance back in the work situation.' Webb goes on to say, however, that in GEC younger managers and many senior managers change their minds about outdoor development once they have seen its effects or gone on the courses themselves.

This book is written to help directors, senior managers, personnel directors, managers, trainers, and employees at all levels in companies and the staff of outdoor development organisations better understand the goals and relevance of outdoor development.

I begin the book with an attempt to place outdoor development in a framework of management development. I then trace the roots of the topic to identify formative influences. Next, I examine the main goals of outdoor development and look at the way organisations design their courses to meet these goals. I discuss debriefing and evaluation and look at testimonials from individual managers and management educators: I then discuss the risk factor in outdoor development. Next I explore some women's issues on the topic. Finally, I look at the areas for further research and draw some conclusions.

In Part II, I present some illustration of how companies use outdoor development. These diverse companies include:

1   American Medical International (AMI), a worldwide health care service company;
2   Provident Mutual Life Assurance Association;
3   Dunlop Limited, the multinational;
4   Plessey Telecommunications Limited;
5   Unigate Dairy Holdings Limited;
6   Haden plc, a construction company;
7   General Electric Company;
8   Securicor, a security organisation;
9   Safeway Foodstores Limited, a multinational grocery chain;
10 Union International Company Limited, a multinational which handles meat from the grazing fields to its own chain of high street shops.

I then review most of the outdoor development organisations in Great Britain and describe the range of courses on offer.

I hope the book will help create a more informed dialogue about the topic but it can be no more than an instructor's firm hand on the shoulder before a parachute jump. The exhilarating plunge into outdoor development is down to the reader.

John Bank

ACKNOWLEDGEMENTS

I am grateful to *many* dedicated outdoor development professionals with whom I've worked closely over the years, particularly Eskdale Outward Bound staff, Roger Putnam and Jerry Bennett; and Stewart Wagstaff, now with the Coventry Education Authority. Others I've met only in gathering data for this book, but I feel a bonding with them in the effort and genuine gratitude for their help.

Likewise, I'm thankful to the hundreds of management students whose experiences of outdoor development formed the raw material for this book. I hope they enjoy the flashbacks in the stories and events set down here and agree with some of the main threads of my argument.

A vote of thanks is also due to my colleagues at the London Business School, the Cranfield School of Management and elsewhere who have helped me to try to make sense of it all. Susan Vinnicombe, colleague and fellow traveller, deserves special mention for suggesting the book. Like most researchers I am always surprised by the openness and generosity of managers who *make* the time to answer a questionnaire or to welcome me into their offices. The book is a visible way of saying 'thanks' as well as delivering the promised feedback. My thanks go to Hugh Butland, a Cranfield MBA, who as a student helped me both collect and analyse data from companies. I also appreciated the invitation to attend an outdoor development conference by the British Institute of Management. A former Cranfield MBA student, Anna Maria Garden, now in a doctoral programme at MIT, should be credited with broadening my knowledge of burn-out with her original research. To meet the publisher's deadline, two secretaries in the Human Resources Group at Cranfield, Mairi Bryce and June Wardill, mounted a special effort. They showered down many more words than appear here. I applaud their speed, skill and energy. My secretary, Susan Dean, finished the manuscript with efficiency, style and good humour. As a member of a dual-career family, I'm grateful for the extra responsibility my wife Jane took with the children while I was off on field trips or chasing interviews for the book or holed up in a corner of our house, writing.

JB

PART I
MAPPING THE CONCEPT

1 FRAMEWORK

We are viewing with increasing suspicion the rush to harness this approach . . . With Cranfield, London, Manchester and Ashridge all having inserted an element of outdoor training in sound courses, do we detect 'customer appeal' as being dominant in the thinking? We will be using Sundridge Park more just to get away from it.

J K Gregory, personnel development manager
The Nestlé Co.

What is outdoor development and how does it fit into traditional management development?

Outdoor development may be very adventurous to the participants who stretch themselves in the challenging activities, yet it is *not adventure* in the usual meaning of the word.

'To me, adventure involves a journey, or a sustained endeavour, in which there are the elements of risk and of the unknown which have to be overcome by the physical skills of the individual,' wrote mountaineer Chris Bonington. 'Furthermore, an adventure is something that an individual chooses to do and where the risk involved is self-imposed and threatens no one but himself'. Bonington then rules out soldiering from his concept of adventure. 'The soldier's adventures and thrills are at the expense of others and part of the thrill of adventure can become the thrill of the hunt. This goes outside my own ground rules'.[1]

Colin J. Mortlock defines adventure education as that which 'uses as a medium those outdoor pursuits which are potentially dangerous. It involves the presentation of a meaningful challenge to people within a framework of safety, in order to give them a deep personal and social awareness'.[2] The emphasis in such an approach is on the individual and the focus is on the physical task rather than on a management development/organisational need, or on the process people go through in outdoor development activities. The adventurer, John Ridgway, who rowed across the Atlantic with Chay Blyth in 1966, has conducted adventure courses for managers. When asked by one of his clients, IBM, to incorporate debriefings and discussions about processes that accompanied the physical tasks, he simply declined to do them or to allow IBM trainers to carry them out. Ridgway's refusal indicates the style of adventure training which would leave out feedback and analysis during the course itself. Review of the adventure activities is down to the individuals in their own time after the outdoor programmes.

In my own eight years of experience in using the outdoors with managers, I have found the review of the processes involved in physical activities to be a constituent element of outdoor development. Without it, the learning is haphazard, the benefits left to chance. My own use of adventure is in sync with that of D.H. Williams, who runs an organisation called Impact Development Training. In Williams's approach, 'adventure is used purely as an educational vehicle, as part of an integrated programme of activities which . . . present frequent opportunities for reflection on experiences and situations occurring within the course . . . in an effort to realise specific objectives . . . in relation to the individual's personal development and the work situation'.[3]

The Leadership Trust over its nine-year history has put greater emphasis on course review and process analysis of its physical activities, cutting back on these activities to provide more room for real learning. The Leadership Trust, for example, no longer runs all-night exercises because these left the men too tired to concentrate on the learning.

Without built-in debriefings to get at the transferable learning and valuable lessons inherent in physical tasks in the outdoors, a programme could become a purely personal adventure. The Dangerous Sports Club begun at Oxford in the late 1970s, for example, had personal impact and value akin to outdoor development programmes for some of its participants. Simon Keeting, one of the club's members, described an expedition the Club made in 1979 to hang-glide from the 19,340 feet high summit of Kilimanjaro. At the end of his report on the experience for which Mr Keeting spent £1,200 of his own money, he observed that had the event been an outdoor development programme for managers:

1 a firm's money, not his own, would have been at risk;
2 the activity would have been better scheduled and more tightly organised with a permit to use the mountain obtained beforehand; and
3 the group would have been accompanied by experts in mountaineering and hang-gliding.

'A lot of the risk and challenge would have been taken out of it; this would have detracted from its value considerably', he said.[4]

The young manager's observation about the risk being diminished by outdoor development is quite correct; however, his supposition that this would have devalued the experience is open to question. On the contrary, a systematic outdoor development programme may well have made the Kilimanjaro expedition the learning experience of a lifetime.

The essential difference between adventure and outdoor development, then, is that in adventure the activity is primary and any learning that results is a by-product, whereas, in outdoor development, the physical event is subordinate to the primary activity, which is the learning about leadership, team building, communications, oneself, others, stress management, decision making.

In the outdoor development programmes at the South West Regional Management Centre, Mick Beeby works to a pedagogy which incorporates this view: the essential characteristics of outdoor development are the use of outdoors, incorporation of process reviews and application of experiential learning methods.[5]

Management development for 'real'

Management development has three goals:

1   to provide knowledge of theory, best practice, technologies and techniques;
2   to foster appropriate positive attitudes; and
3   to develop practical specific skills.

The traditional way of imparting knowledge through lectures, readings, assignments, discussions, tests, etc. are well tried in schooling and form a normal part of management education. Case studies add a new dimension for knowledge transmission. But attitudinal change is often needed if a manager is to act in harmony with the knowledge of management science. A set of attitudes is required for managers which includes self-confidence, trust in colleagues, a participative exercise of authority, a readiness to act, a willingness to lead and inspire teamwork, the capability to change, the eagerness to take responsibility and the ability to delegate. These types of attitudes are shaped by positive and powerful emotional experiences which are fostered by interpersonal activities.

Experiential learning, then, becomes a vital component of effective management development. It is a process 'which begins with the experience, followed by reflection, discussion, analysis and evaluation of the experience. The assumption is that we seldom learn from experience unless we assess the experience, assigning our own meaning in terms of our own goals, aims, ambitions and expectations'.[6]

It is precisely such an experiential learning model that is used in outdoor development. The circular learning pattern developed by Kolb[7] and shown in Figure 1 is appropriate as a model for learning in outdoor development.

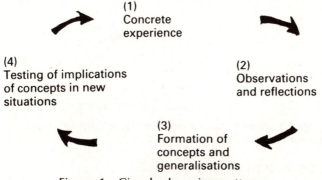

(1)
Concrete
experience

(4)
Testing of implications
of concepts in new
situations

(2)
Observations
and reflections

(3)
Formation of
concepts and
generalisations

Figure 1   Circular learning pattern

Source: Kolb, D.A. *et el., Organisational Psychology: An Experiential Approach,* Prentice-Hall, 1971.

Further inkling into how Outdoor Development fits into a managerial skills framework can be gathered from Waters' analysis[8] (see Figure 2). Outdoor development would fit into the classification he labels insight skills in quadrant 3. These *insight skills* include working in groups, dealing with ambiguity and change, building trust and negotiating.

Context skills include goal setting, work planning, designing controls, building commitment. *Wisdom* embraces: charisma, entrepreneurship, strategy formulation. Finally, *practical skills* include performance appraising, report writing, active listening.

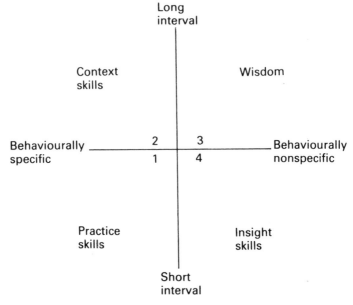

Figure 2   Managerial skills framework

Source: Waters, James A., 'Managerial Skill Development', *Academy of Management Review,* vol. 5 no. 3, pp. 449-453.

Outdoor action learning

Far from the fanciful images it is sometimes given, outdoor development has a real-world focus with a natural skills orientation. Not surprisingly, this is an orientation necessary for managers in the last decades of this century. As one international observer put it: 'The contribution of management development that is most important is the pragmatism and people skills its participants develop – mainly through contact with the real world'.[9]

Foy makes a strong case for 'action learning' and gives her own personal testimony. 'I am devoted to action learning, exposure to others from outside cultures, informal shoulder-rubbing, and so on, with the best of management development, in the form of risk taking, accountability, and access to older, wiser managers who can share their insights about organisation . . . [10]

There is an element of 'action learning' in the model for outdoor development, whereby managers 'learn by doing the thing'.[11] The principles of 'action learning' were taken up by the EEC's Foundation for Management Development (EFMD) when it stated: 'New approaches in educational technology for large audiences, action research and action learning . . . should be broadly experimented with and promoted'.[12] These principles can easily be applied to outdoor managerial development. At the heart of action learning is the ability to extract from the new task itself a sustainable desire to know what one is trying to do, what is preventing this and what resources can be found to get it done by overcoming the obstacles. Usually, the process requires the help of a small number of people who are also on the same quest.

To the people who summed up his work with the simplistic phrase, 'learning by doing', Professor Revans said that it was rather 'learning to learn-by-doing with and from others who are also learning to learn-by-doing'.[13] The focus is, then, not on the knowledge of the teacher, but rather on the experiences and the needs of the learners. In particular, the outdoor development programme emphasises one of the options of action learning whereby an unfamiliar problem is studied in an unfamiliar setting.

The physical tasks at the core of outdoor development courses, whether they be abseiling a rockface, climbing a mountain peak or navigating rapids in canoes, are real tasks which present real problems to real people in real time with real constraints. Unlike simulations and case studies, the physical tasks are so designed that the manager will experience the practical outcome of his own actions or decisions, thereby creating a learning process which could lead him to modify his behaviour or options. As such, the physical tasks in the outdoor development courses, dependent as they are on small group work, constitute 'action learning' experiences which stand on their own.

The managers in action course run by the Brathay Hall

Trust claims to turn out managers 'who are able to act more positively and flexibly as managers of groups, communicators, decision makers and team members'. The Trust's seven-day course has a skills focus for practising managers. The course follows the theories of John Adair, the founder of action-centred leadership, which has enjoyed wide application throughout British industry.[14] According to the action-centred leadership model, an efficient manager needs to have:

1   technical competence to manage the technology of the job;
2   knowledge of the functional area of management; and
3   a cluster of management skills required to motivate people to work for corporate goals.[15]

Testing managerial skills

The skills area is most relevant to outdoor development. What, then, are the specific managerial skills which can be practical and reinforced through outdoor activities? A list of these skills would include:

1   observing;
2   selecting pertinent data;
3   diagnosing problems;
4   formulating solutions;
5   deciding;
6   communicating; and
7   motivating.

Across the spectrum, the physical activities can range from simple rock climbing, where groups achieve goals, to survival exercises, where individuals are left on their own to find routes while living off the land. It is quite obvious that the physical activity must be suited to the desired outcomes.

For example, one of the desired outcomes of the Leadership Trust's management training is to help a student learn ways of handling and controlling himself

effectively even under pressure. The training is reinforced by a tutor attached to every six to ten students
who in effect provides a model example of such control
in his own behaviour. The tutor also holds the safety of
the group and establishes the integrity and boundary of

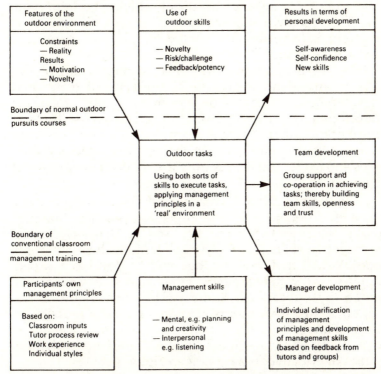

Figure 3 Linking the outdoor environment with management
development – a basic model

Source: Creswick, C., and Williams, R., *Using the Outdoors for
Management Development and Team Building,* The Food and
Tobacco Industry Training Board, Gloucester, 1979.

the group in which the member can become freer and
freer to express himself. The tutor creates a membrane of
safety and support for the group. He makes sure that
each person has at least one, usually two, opportunities
of leading the group and experiencing support.

Each group, in turn, tests itself out in three physical
activities: sub-aqua diving, rock climbing and canoeing.

The physical activities themselves comprise only 8 per cent of the course content, but they are crucial because they are used to wrench people out of their normal patterns of behaviour and mind sets. As Michael Price, executive course director of Leadership Trust, explained: 'The physical activity is a powerful vehicle. It is important that it be totally real because then you get real emotion, real fear, high anxiety, high or low morale, real aggression and real learning'.[16]

Effective programmes that take managers out of the classroom and into the outdoors should result in personal development, team development and manager development.[17] These outdoor programmes use tasks as focal points where there is a convergence of inputs from management training which include managerial principles and skills, and inputs from the outdoor environment (see Figure 3).

As with physical skills, managerial skills are developed through frequent use and reflective practice. Various participative methods can be used to sharpen diverse managerial skills. Hawrylyshyn[18] argues that although participative methods can be used to develop a broad range of skills, they are most effective over a very narrow range of applications. Some participative methods are simply better than others at giving a person practice in these managerial skills. An attempt to illustrate the range of application of participative methods together with their peaks of effectiveness is made in Figure 4.

Following this insight, if a company wanted to develop in its managers the skill of observing, it would get best results from fieldwork activities. To develop the ability of its managers to select data, the company would have the most success with the incident method. There would be little point to using the case study method for developing either of these two skills because in that method the observing and data selection are done beforehand by the case writer, not the management student.

The strength of the case study lies in its aptness for diagnosing problems and formulating solutions. A well

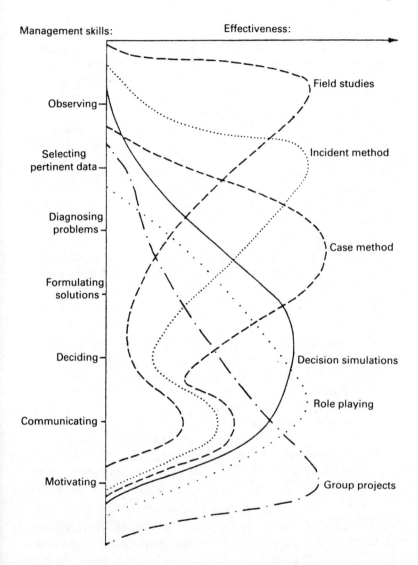

Figure 4   Effectiveness of participative methods

Source: Hawrylyshyn, B., 'Preparing Managers for International Operations', *The Business Quarterly,* Autumn 1967, p. 31.

written case study is a testing ground for competing managerial judgements on concrete issues. Yet case studies have their drawbacks. 'When it comes to learning how to make sound decisions, the case method is far from ideal because there are no penalties for proposing wrong decisions; as there are no real consequences, solutions can be proposed light-heartedly'.[19]

On the contrary, the action-based case studies in outdoor development activities are very real and the penalties for wrong decisions painful; the consequence of bad judgements can be as real as being lost in a cold rainstorm at the edge of a dark forest.

The Food, Drink and Tobacco Industry Training Board in its several years' experience with outdoor development training has emphasised the objective of managing change and uncertainty. 'Managers apply their skills to a range of tasks which are quite different to those they face at work but which are challenging and real', stated a seminal report on development training from the Training Board.[20]

> The results of their action are immediately apparent, providing clear evidence of their performance and a basis for feedback, questioning and experiment. Although the outdoor tasks are not *normal*, they are inescapably *real*. Managing an outdoor situation is like managing life – it is full of unpredictable events and people, a result has to be achieved and there are only limited resources and time available. Because the tasks are so different from the normal work situation, the underlying management processes are laid bare.[21]

Chris Bonington is a believer in the reality of the outdoors to sharpen managerial action. Executive decision making, participative leadership, team building, the management of uncertainty, motivation, dealing with industrial relations (a threatened strike by the Sherpas) are all part of the life and death reality of a major mountain climbing expedition. These aspects of management are as real as the logistics planning and stock control for which Bonington used computer programming. He feels that in climbing Everest in 1975, he encountered nearly 'every type of management problem one could think of'.[22] His many Himalayan expeditions, while light years beyond the scope of outdoor development for managers, have all been an extreme confirmation of the power of the outdoors as a vehicle for managing uncertainty.

2 ROOTS

We would consider using Outdoor Development if senior management declared a policy of 'True Darwinism' within the organisation.

A. Goodenough, Avon Overseas Ltd

The managers in rough clothing with maps in hand converged on an old trunk half hidden in the middle of the forest. They opened it to find ropes and a pulley and the directive to use the equipment to get the entire team across a ravine in two hours. 'This is a "WOS-B"! ' said one manager who had been an army officer. The other younger managers did not know what the word meant, nor did they understand the strong emotion behind his statement. They were unaware of the 'WOS-B' root of outdoor development.

'WOS-B' stands for War Office Selection Board which deals with officer promotion in the Army in the first instance and in the second for challenging outdoor problems like the ones used by the War Office Selection

Board for assessment of the men before it. The Navy has a corresponding Board called the Admiralty Interview Board which uses similar group exercises to sort out candidates.

There are at least six roots to outdoor development as used today with managers. They are:

1 the military;
2 outdoor sports;
3 Outward Bound;
4 outdoor education through the school system;
5 other youth activities, such as Scouts and the Duke of Edinburgh Award, etc.; and
6 organisational development (OD).

The military

The use of the outdoors for training by the military goes back to the earliest days of military training. There is no record that Hannibal first trained his troops in the Alps before crossing them, but he might have. Today, all branches of the military use the outdoors to train their fighting men, to develop their officers and to select out élite corps.

The selection course for the British Parachute Regiment, for example, which eliminates two-thirds of all candidates who attempt it, gives the men less than two hours to complete a ten-mile battle march, carrying 30lb packs, 20lb of webbing and a 10lb rifle. After struggling through mud and water and hillsides, the men are kept awake all night digging trenches, doing exercises and fending off instructors who creep up on them and attempt to steal weapons and equipment. At dawn, the candidates run a six-and-a-half mile stretcher race across difficult country in teams of eight, each man carrying 175lb on his shoulders. They must then go round the assault course three times in under seven-and-a-half minutes and complete the steeplechase within 18 minutes. Finally, they have to carry telegraph poles over rough terrain in less than 15 minutes and do a 14-mile march over harsh landscape. The Para leadership maintains they are not out to break men but 'to make them', to find the man 'who doesn't quit, who has the robustness of mind to keep going when everyone else falls.'

While outdoor development programmes have neither the rigour nor the 'selection intent' of such military activities, they do draw on some similar activities, such as an assault course or challenges like crossing a deep chasm with ropes and a pulley. Dipping into military handbooks for physical tasks and outdoor exercises which can be used on outdoor development courses is quite legitimate, provided these activities are modified to take account of the age and physical fitness of the managers; and the primacy of learning over the physical task in outdoor development.

Outdoor sports

Outdoor sports, such as mountaineering, sailing, white-water canoeing, caving, diving, orienteering and running, continue to feed the outdoor development movement for managers like underground streams feed a spring. As each of these sports has rewritten its own history with accomplishments that push back frontiers of human striving and with new techniques and equipment, there have been spin-offs for the outdoor development movement. Outdoor development borrows heavily from the sports and is interested in the techniques and equipment and in making participation in the outdoor activities safer and more meaningful. Usually, the physical instructors for outdoor development courses are accomplished at one or more outdoor sports and this reinforces benefits derived from the sports.

At times, the mere presence of the instructors, fit in mind and body, among a group of over-indulgent, unfit managers, generates some soul-searching. Doubters of the ability men and women have to regain fitness and a love for physical exercise should examine the phenomenon of running in America. A decade ago only three million Americans engaged in running as a sport and the image of the beer-drinking, TV-watching, sedentary American male was widespread. Today, over 30 million Americans run as a sport, many of them participating in demanding marathon running, 26 miles 385 yards (42.195 km).

Not only does outdoor development draw on outdoor sports for many of its physical activities; the thrust of using the outdoors for managers among enthusiasts for outdoor sport can awaken commitment to a lifestyle of more demanding physical exertion in a way akin to a religious retreat reawakening religious fervour and practice. There is a strong tradition that argues for the transferability of energy and discipline from outdoor sports to work life. One of the most recent testimonials is in the portrayal of a man named Bob West in Tracy Kidder's documentary book, *The Soul of a New Machine*. West builds computers and sails like a man possessed:

> West was at the helm, the tiller in both hands, riding the waves; he was standing under a swaying lantern in the cabin studying the chart, he was nimbly climbing out on to the foredeck to wrestle in a jib and replace it with a smaller one. And when the captain decided to make for shelter, very late that night, at a little harbour with a passage into it that was twisting, narrow and full of tide, it was West, standing up in the bow, who spotted each unlighted channel marker and guided them safely in.[23]

West is introduced to the reader as a good man in a storm who did not sleep for four nights in a row, and later is seen as the leader of a project team racing to create a new and revolutionary computer. He is seen as a high-powered manager who returns to sailing for relaxation, a reduction of tension and inner renewal; the way many managers today are turning to outdoor sport for survival.

Outward Bound

There are 34 Outward Bound schools in 17 countries today

and their ongoing influence on outdoor development is considerable.[24] The founder of Outward Bound was Kurt Hahn, a German-Jewish educator, who earlier developed the Salem School in Germany in 1920 as an antithesis of the authoritarian German schools of the time. His opposition to the Nazi régime won him a prison sentence in 1933, but influential friends got him released and out of Germany. He went to Scotland where he founded Gordonstoun school in 1934. His philosophy of education stressed the development of a student's inner resources as well as intellectual challenge. He trained his school boys in mountain and ocean rescue. At the outbreak of the Second World War, Hahn helped to set up a school for British merchant mariners at Aberdovey, Wales, specialising in survival training. The school was named 'Outward Bound' and that became the name for the international Outward Bound movement dedicated to Hahn's philosophy of education. The Aberdovey school is now one of the leading Outward Bound schools in management education and in the rough economic climate of Britain in the 1980s is still in the survival business.

Outward Bound has always concentrated on courses for youth and has funding from industry for such work. Its involvement in management education, according to Ian Fothergill, director of the Outward Bound Trust and formerly principal of Outward Bound at Aberdovey, is a long-term commitment. Roger Putnam, principal of the Outward Bound school at Eskdale, has carried his commitment to management education far enough to purchase a stone mansion near the school's entrance for the education of managers. 'Personal fulfilment and character building can only aid the managerial role,' said a Cranfield MBA student making the link between the course and his job. But Outward Bound is reaching far beyond its own roots to deal with management development in all its many facets.

The American Outward Bound schools have made a good deal of the running with outdoor development in conjunction with business schools and universities and, at times, private organisations like the Center for Creative Leadership.[25]

Outdoor education

Outdoor development has roots that are seldom acknowledged in outdoor education, which is a term now widely accepted as covering educational activities concerned with living, moving and learning out-of-doors. These activities include camping and residential experiences and skills requiring physical endeavour and observation of the environment. Outdoor education, then, is not a subject, but it provides opportunities to complement learning planned by the school. Its goals are to instil respect for oneself through the meeting of challenge and adventure, for others through group experience and shared decision making, and for the natural environment through direct experience.

The focus in outdoor education is on personal development of the young students and the outdoors is seen as a powerful pedagogy for teaching self-reliance, cooperation, confidence, imagination, inventiveness and a capacity for sustained physical endeavour – all of which virtues are important in the work and in the building of a strong society.[26]

Between 1907 and 1921, local education authorities were empowered to provide outdoor activities for students through vacation schools, vacation classes and school camps. By 1928, fifteen LEAs were running school camps and in 1931 camping was introduced as a part of teacher training at one college. The Norwood Report in 1943 argued that there was 'moral strength' to be derived from involving young people in adventurous land- and water-based open-air tasks.

Outdoor education grew rapidly from 1960 when only a couple of LEAs had residential courses for outdoor activities to 1970 when LEAs ran about 400 residential centres. In addition, schools have acquired huts, cottages, disused railway stations, village schools and camps. They have also enlisted 300 field study bases and over 500 outdoor pursuit centres and a range of residential accommodation provided by voluntary, private or commercial organisations to help achieve the goals of outdoor education. Social development was one of the goals which encompassed relating to their teachers in a more humane and approachable manner and giving the non-academic student a long tether to achieve.

An HMI survey of outdoor education and short-stay residential experience published in 1982 concluded:

> There has been a continuing and increasing demand, from all types of schools and colleges, for places in LEA short-stay residential outdoor centres and a considerable growth in the number of centres. This development in the education service during the last 20 years is all the more remarkable since generally it has been achieved in the absence of central legislation or funding.[27]

The growth in the use of the outdoors for management development parallels this growth in outdoor education. Although the learning in outdoor development for managers is at an adult/organisational level, it shares some of the confidence-building and team-work experiences used in outdoor education. Regardless of age, the outdoors provides powerful learning to the willing student.

Outdoor development also benefits from a spin-off from the growth in outdoor education which created career structures for men and women who share an equal passion for outdoor pursuits and education. The new breed of physical instructors in schools across the country are likely to be people with degrees who have come up the educational route. Whereas before, the Outward Bound instructor, for example, might have been a fitter from a car factory who had a passion for climbing which eventually took over and led him to a full-time position in an Outward Bound school, the new Outward Bound instructor was likely to have been a teacher specialising in outdoor activities. Some would argue that this was a double-edged change. The educational qualifications may have made the new breed of physical instructors more conversant with the academic questions of managers, but it might also have stripped them of invaluable business and industrial experience which would have helped them build bridges back to the work place.

Youth activities

A number of youth programmes, such as the Boy Scouts, Girl Guides, the Duke of Edinburgh's Award scheme, the Sail Training Association, the Dartmouth Challenge, Operation Raleigh, etc., provide meaningful introductions to learning from the outdoors which young men and women carry with them into the adult world of business and industry. The focus of such youth activity is often 'character-building', but youths readily cope with the moral expectations adults place on them and they manage to have memorable experiences despite parental demands. The lasting imprint of these experiences is quite remarkable. Most people remember what they were doing when they learned that President John Kennedy was assassinated because the shock and drama of the event heightened their memory to create an indelible moment. In a similar manner, the drama of outdoor events, like abseiling a 200-foot cliff, heightens the moment and makes vivid memories and learning easy to recall.

For managers who as youths have had memorable outdoor experiences, adult development programmes link back to the reservoir of good feelings and powerful remembrances. Outdoor development builds on, but also creates, its own series of vivid, indelible memories. Evidence of this was volunteered to me in a discussion with Patrick Dolan, secretary of the National Society of Quality Circles. He recalled a week-end at Celmi as an ICI manager and said he could remember every detail of the experience six years on, whereas other management courses since then blurred in his memory or were totally forgotten.

Organisational development

The overarching field of social technology, of organisation change and development referred to as organisational development (OD) is a significant root of outdoor development for managers. The impact of OD principles and technology on industry and business has fed the growth of outdoor development.

Over the years, industrial psychologists made their most important contribution to the success of business by developing technologies for selecting and training employees. A weakness inherent in selection technologies has been their preoccupation with a criterion of effectiveness which reflects a company's past success rather than its future requirements. A weakness of traditional training methods is their poor results in attempts to alter human behaviour. Classic examples are human relations training programmes with a heavy knowledge basis which simply fail to change the behaviour of supervisors in any significant way. When major changes of behaviour are achieved, they often clash head-on with the leadership or organisational climate and the transplants fail to take root in such alien soil.[28]

These technologies of selection and training have not helped companies meet the demands of 'the third wave', the micro-technology revolution which will require whole industries to make radical changes and initiate massive restructuring.[29]

A further failure of traditional selection and training methods is that their focus on the quality of individuals fails to take into account the fact that organisations are more than the sum total of the individuals who work in them. They are rather complex social systems with intricate inter-relations between inputs, processes, internal environment and outputs. To focus simply on the individual through selection and training is to ignore the organisation as a total system.

OD, then, is a response to the demands of an organisation as a total system. Its techniques to solve organisational problems and to meet organisational needs now comprise an expanding technology for interviewing in changing and developing organisations.

OD employs a model of change based on Kurt Lewin's theory[30] which has a three-stage process of:

1   *unfreezing*: a decrease in the strength of old attitudes, values or behaviours, resulting from informa-

tion or experiences which disconfirm one's perception of self, others or events;

2 *changing:* the development of new attitudes, values or behaviours through identification or internalisation; and

3 *refreezing:* the stabilisation of change at a new equilibrium state through supporting changes in reference groups, culture or organisational policy and structure.

Each technology used in OD may be evaluated according to its power to effect change at all of its stages.

Into this conceptual framework, the varied technologies of OD can be fitted. T-groups, or sensitivity training, is an OD technology which consists of a wide-ranging assortment of experience-based training. The goals, content and training styles of T-groups are divergent and so are the outcomes. But the primacy they have given to experiential learning has prepared the ground for the different, experience-based learning found in outdoor development.

Team development or team building is another commonly used and powerful OD technology which directly relates to outdoor development. 'The objective of team development is the removal of immediate barriers to group effectiveness and the development of self-sufficiency in managing group process and problems in the future'.[31]

Beer distinguishes four separate models for team development:

1 *the goal-setting model* where goals influence individual and group behaviour;

2 *the interpersonal model* with its underlying assumption that people with interpersonal skills can function better as a team. The focus is on shared feelings, mutual supportiveness, non-evaluative communication, trust and confidence, encouraged risk taking and, ultimately, higher commitment to group goals;

3 *the role model.* A 'role' is a set of expectations and behaviours associated with a given position in a social system.[32] The elements of this definition

include: *role expectation* – the set of structurally given normative demands and responsibilities associated with a position; *role concept* – the individual's own definition of how a person in his position is supposed to think and act; and *role performance* – the person's actual behaviour as it relates to his position.[33]

A group, therefore, is a set of overlapping roles and much of the behaviour in a work group can be understood in terms of individuals' perceptions of these roles.

4   *the managerial grid model.* Blake and Mouton[34] have created a team development meeting based on their grid laboratory. In this approach, each team spends a week applying the grid framework to an examination of the way it operated. There is a heavy use of instruments before this meeting by individuals. In the end, the team tries to reach a consensus on its ideal operations and its actual operating. Needs are identified and plans for both individual and team development are made.

Team building on outdoor development courses generally has most in common with the goal-setting model or the inter-personal model, although the role model or the grid model could also be drawn on in team building using the outdoors. Yet team building, vital as it is for managers, is only one of a half-dozen outdoor development goals.

3 GOALS

Having undertaken leadership training for some years, we were not satisfied with the exercises used to illustrate the concepts which were seen as being not very relevant. We therefore decided to run outdoor adventure-based, learning exercises which have been conceived and developed and are run entirely in house.

(A. J. Frost, training and development manager, Safeway Foodstores Ltd)

Outdoor development courses can be used to achieve the following goals:

1 self-development through personal audit;
2 an antidote or cure for burn-out;
3 an experience of team building;
4 attitudinal change in the assessment of self and of others;
5 the development of leadership;
6 a living workshop for communication skills; and

7   an experience of dealing with change and uncertainty.

Self-development

Given a set of novel and demanding exercises, the participant will dig deep into his own resources to find hidden strengths and uncover weaknesses. The aim is to effect a confidence-building experience based on extending oneself. In the dramatic outdoor scene, the course member begins to realise that many of the limitations he feels are artificial and self-imposed. Quite naturally he takes stock of his own level of health and fitness measured against his peers and staff members. It can be a salutary experience for an over-indulgent executive to abseil a rockface with an amazingly fit climber or for a timid manager to brave the white water of rapids with a fearless colleague.

In this area of self-development, the physical environment is used to stimulate personal risk taking, exposure and the exploration of one's own rules, habits and constraints. Self-development is seen as the unearthing of personal abilities and capacities which makes the person as manager more autonomous.[35]

One of the personal objectives is developing a commitment to better physical fitness. There is an underlying belief in the real link between physical fitness and mental alertness, high morale, motivation and general effectiveness. It is felt that the outdoor experience may prompt a participant to develop a régime of regular exercise which is tailored to his personality, lifestyle, age, current level of fitness and personal motivation. There is a potential pay-off for both the person and his company here in all areas of work, particularly in stressful and demanding situations.

Although a modern manager may work in a high tech office, he still lives in a caveman's body. His body simply took millions of years to evolve into a form capable of primitive survival for fighting or for fleeing. It needs vigorous daily exercise. It needs to move out of the danger rhythm it goes into when under threat and to relax in a vegetative rhythm where no adrenalin flows.

The communion with nature stimulated by outdoor development opens up reflections on a deeper interior life. As Henry David Thoreau put it: 'I went into the woods because I wished to live deliberately, to confront the essential facts of life and to see if I could not learn what it had to teach, and not, when I came to die, discover that I had not lived'.[36]

An antidote to burn out

The outdoor development experience can also be an antidote to burn out. New research in America has broadened the categories for burn out to go beyond professional athletes and people in the performing arts, where it originated in the 1930s, and beyond the 'helping professions', where the concept became popular in the 1970s, focusing on doctors and mental health workers, soldiers, policemen and airline personnel to encompass business men and women and many others. 'Burn out' is a state many people find themselves in when they have made intense efforts with few or no visible results. As a consequence, they feel angry, helpless, caged and spent. Managers are subjected to this sense of exhaustion and futility and to a higher level of stress.[37]

There is at present a number of descriptions of burn out. Maslach who has produced a 'burn out inventory' defines burn-out as a syndrome of emotional exhaustion, depersonalisation, and lowered productivity.[38]

Freudenberger describes burn out as 'to deplete oneself; to exhaust one's physical and mental resources; to wear oneself out by excessively striving to reach some unrealistic expectation imposed by one's self or by the values of society'.[39]

Limiting burn out to professionals, Cherniss calls it 'a process in which a previously committed professional disengages from his or her work in response to stress and strain experienced in the job.'[40] Behavioural symptoms are encompassed in Veninga and Spradley's definition of burn out as 'a debilitating psychological condition brought about by unrelieved work stress which results in

– depleted energy reserves
– lowered resistance to illness
– increased dissatisfaction and pessimism
– increased absenteeism and inefficiency.[41]

Levinson declares that 'many contemporary managerial situations provide the perfect breeding ground for cases of burnout'.[42] The danger of burn out reaches even the chief executive, according to Ginsberg.

> The crawl or climb to the top has been, in a substantial number of cases, so tough, tension-filled and debilitating, that once there, the base has been firmly laid for a good case of being burned out. Also, when finally at the top, the pressures to prove to others and one's self that it was indeed worth it and that one is the best man for the office; to put one's individual stamp as quickly as possible on the orga-nization; to be strong, dynamic, decisive, innovative and right – all serve to produce additional tensions which in time bring on the burnout syndrome . . . Even if a solid base for being burned out were not established in the climb to the top, the normal pressures on the top man, the way we expect decisions to be made, the heroic, charismatic styles we expect, and the time/tension demands that orga-nizations place, all mean that the top man may be facing the beginnings or advanced symptoms of being burned out.[43]

Tubesings defines burn out in three powerful words as a 'personal energy crisis'[44] Potter includes this essential aspect of burn out in his description of a burnt-out person as one who 'cannot muster enough energy to participate in life' or someone for whom 'the vital driving force has become a whimper'.[45] Freudenberger calls burn out a 'depletion of the individual's resources, an attrition of his vitality, energy and ability to function'.[46] The state of the art on burn out is nearly as uncharted as that of outdoor development. Empirical studies are missing in both and assumptions and descriptions hold sway. But a relationship between the two phenomena exists and outdoor development is already being recommended by people-focused companies to counteract burn out. In the real world people do not wait for the social scientists to define neatly and operationalise definitions of burn out and gather data on the phenomenon before trying to deal with it.

Outdoor development training programmes with their combination of physical challenge and personal reflection can be apt prescriptions for coping with stress and burn out. Freudenberger recommends that companies deal with these problems by sending managers to workshops and seminars and other off-site physical activities where they have opportunities to release pent-up frustrations and renew themselves.

Just as self-development need not be a solitary quest, and can be strengthened by relationships with others, counteracting burn out need not be a solo activity. Here again, the mutual support established on outdoor development management programmes and the sense of community can be beneficial.

Team building

With stunning superiority the McLaren team propelled Niki Lauda and team mate Alain Prost to finish 1st and 2nd in the Grand Prix at Kalami. The team, among other feats, changed all four tyres on Lauda's car in eight-and-a-half seconds.

Team building has always been an objective of success-ful organisations. It is well known that one of the strengths of the Special Air Service Regiment (SAS) is rooted in the way that organisation builds its teams, carefully maximis-ing each person's strengths and compensating for his weaknesses. The technology required to achieve an SAS objective is generally learned after the team has been formed; in the management world, technology is learned first. Whether the man who knows the technology and is put in charge will be able to weld a team together is often left to chance. Companies do make appeals to team work. One of the more bizarre examples of team building occurred when the manager of the US-based IBM sales unit with 100 people rented a sports stadium in New Jersey for an evening. In front of their spouses and children and some top executives, all members of the sales team ran through the players' tunnel on to the field as their names were flashed on an electronic scoreboard while the crowd cheered.

Another approach to team work, more in keeping with British culture, appeared in an Outward Bound brochure.

> The anchor is weighed, the sails unfolded to catch the wind and the vessel sets out to meet the challenges of the open sea. It is outward bound. The success or failure of its voyage rests not only on the skills of the individuals and the crew, but also on their ability to work together as a well-motivated and stable team through routine manoeuvres and moments of crisis.

The parallel is then rather simplistically drawn between sailing and business activity.

> Such team-work also plays an integral part in the success of the modern business enterprise but is often obscured by the familiarity, pressures and stress of the working environment.

> Outward Bound creates the opportunity for individuals to learn to work together as a team and to meet the challenges presented by the outdoors.

> What participants learn is more than seamanship, rock climbing or canoeing, they learn that each of these activities is a shared experience which depends on co-operation and the assistance of others for success.

They learn that being part of a team is as demanding as leading it and that individual achievement can be magnified through team-work.

In less dramatic ways, most successful companies devote some time to team building, team working and team maintenance.

It is a great benefit to most firms to have people working in a strongly welded team as a corporate entity rather than simply as a group. Yet managers at all levels can easily feel lost in the organisation and isolated from others. The team-work celebrated in 'Theory Z'[47] is often sorely lacking in British and American firms. Two consultants in a new study of 42 of America's best run companies, in *In Search of Excellence*,[48] argue that the best managers value action above all else, a spirit of 'do it, fix it, try it'. The writers draw heavily on the work of social scientist, Ernest Becker, who documents the essential 'dualism' of people to want both to be part of a team and to be recognised individually.[49] Outdoor development training focuses on the first need, while companies must tend to both. The Leadership Trust, for example, states as one of its four overall objectives, 'to develop the ability to build and harness cohesive teams to achieve common objectives'.

Most outdoor development programmes aim to make participants aware of the need to understand the forces at work within groups and between groups of people. They try to develop in groups: shared goals; the realisation that the knowledge and skills of each member are needed to attain its goals; a joint feeling of responsibility for the attainment of goals; and a strong desire to operate as a team.

The outdoor development exercises attempt to clear blockages to effective team work. Among the common blockages are: the wrong structure, poor training, low motivation, poor controls, inappropriate leadership style, bad planning, unclear goals, and uncertain rewards.

Within the span of a few days outdoor activities teams can be led through identifiable stages. Stage one might be called the *me first* stage. In this stage people are rather self-absorbed. They talk together but are filled with their individual concerns and opinions. They know very little about each other's needs, knowledge, skills. There is no common concern for each other and no shared view on what has to be done or how to go about it. What leadership that emerges is often egocentric and fails to assess the abilities within the group. In a 'mountain rescue' exercise, for example, a self-appointed leader failed to discover that a member of his group had been in the army medical corps, knew exactly how to treat the injured climber but shyly held back as the group went from one blunder to another.

Another identifiable stage of team development can be called *the king and his court stage.* A leader takes charge of the group and organises it under his tight control. He is the focal point of the group and makes the decisions. He distributes parts to others in the limited roles he defines for them and coordinates the parts into a whole. For rather straightforward, simple tasks, this style of team management does work. But the 'king'-styled leader cannot handle complicated tasks; he soon suffers from system overload and simply cannot make all the complicated decisions quickly enough. The members of the group – his court – lose energy and the goal often eludes them. The next stage of an effective team is the *half-way there* stage. During this stage the team starts to get to grips with working together. Interpersonal relationship issues, methods of joint working and even the principles of participation come into play.

The final stage is that of a *fully developed team.* At this stage leadership is determined more by the situation than by the force of a single leader's personality – the role is often shared or rotated to best suit the situation. The fluidity and flexibility of the team's operation is one of its strengths. An open exchange among the members is common as they go to the heart of the issues and deal with substantive matters and problems. A synergy develops within the group as people's abilities and talents combine to give the team a power greater than the sum of its individual parts.

Jerry Bennett, an instructor from Eskdale Outward

Bound who enjoys working with managers, tries to achieve fifteen qualities with the teams he builds. These are:

1 *Good communications* within the team and with others outside the team.
2 *Active listening* where members of the team learn to really hear what each is saying.
3 *Self-knowledge,* where team members openly recognise their own strengths and weaknesses.
4 *High trust,* in which the members share a common purpose and trust each other. Energy is spent clarifying facts, deciding on the best methods of solving problems and exploring alternatives. They do not seek to bluff, trap or score off each other; nor do they distort, withhold, or manipulate information and ideas to suit individual goals.
5 *Willingness to use help* – a readiness to turn to others both inside and outside the team is developed.
6 *Cooperation* is the watchword both in joint problem solving and in sharing workloads.
7 *Supportive help* – an umbrella of supportive relationships is extended over team members, subordinates and superiors.
8 *Collaboration* – a spirit of collaboration within the team and with other teams replaces destructive competition.
9 *Creative conflict* is fostered instead of dysfunctional conflict.
10 *Open leadership issues.* The pecking order is eliminated from team work; rivalries for leadership diminish as responsibilities are shared and accepted.
11 *Meaningful meetings* – consensus not compromise prevails in group decision making.
12 *Action* – things get done, there is little waste of energy.
13 *Good decision making* based on facts not opinions takes place.

14 *Goals known and achieved* – individuals and the team have the satisfaction of realising objectives.

15 *Reviews* of both task and process. The team is interested in *what* it is accomplishing (task) and also *how* it is working together (process).

Bennett's approach is an ambitious effort but one that is a sure-fire way of building a team. Not surprisingly, as experts point out, a person needs, at one and the same time, to be a conforming member of a winning team and a star in his own right.

Assessment

Assessment is an ethical issue in management education. Business schools, as a policy, do not provide companies with specific feedback on individual management student performance. Such feedback could compromise lecturers and would certainly be regarded as a threat by executive students. By setting to one side such assessment, the business school creates a protective environment where the management student feels safe to explore issues, techniques, skills, without the feeling that his company's personnel director is lurking somewhere in the back-ground, waiting to talk with the lecturers, to take a measure of his performance, to compare him with his peers, to weigh his promotion potential.

This ethic is usually adopted by the organisation in-volved in outdoor development management education, particularly when such activities are joint ventures involv-ing, say, an Outward Bound school and a university's business studies department. Hence, the assessment that goes on during outdoor development management courses is not usually to help the sponsoring company's personnel department size up particular managers, but rather to foster self-assessment and a safe environment in which course members are free to evaluate each other's performance and to offer helpful appraisal of behaviour; as two experienced trainers in this field suggest:

Our objectives for the programme were severalfold: For the participant as manager, we would provide a series of opportunities for him to take a complete view of himself as a resource and to extend his capacities to meet a complex variety of managerial situations. We would provide him with opportunities to see himself as others see him and to reflect upon those views, adapting his own behaviour if he so chooses.[50]

An exception to this general approach to forego assessment during outdoor development courses is made by Dunlop International and will be examined in detail later.

Whether the course participants are undertaking a management course with an experience-based outdoor learning module or are on a contract company course, there is bound to be reassessment of others. The sudden change from the classroom or company offices or factory floor to the rockface or the rapids forces participants to evaluate each other in new role sets with entirely new demands.

The development of leadership

The latest company-based research in America argues convincingly for an exploration of leadership by managers. The chief executives of the most successful US companies require leadership skills – 'a strong leader (or two) seemed to have had a lot to do with making the company excellent in the first place'.[51] The great leaders leave behind a legacy that their successors must protect. The leadership task of the chief executive is 'to manage the values of the organisation'.[52] They demand high quality in their product and employee participation in their operations. They ask for their employees' ideas and 'treat them like adults', allowing talented people 'long tethers' for experimenting.[53]

All experience-based outdoor training for managers has the development of leadership as one of its objectives.

The Leadership Trust, for example, in its promotional material sets out its philosophy of leadership, which is quite prescriptive.

> Leadership is both a science and an art. The scientific or 'head' aspect refers to its principles, methods and functions. It involves problem solving, establishing objectives, planning, organising and decision making. The art or 'heart' aspect refers to the intangible human factors. These are personal qualities, personal power, morale, motivation and the vital areas of human relations, such as trust and integrity. *Leadership starts with knowing and controlling oneself so that one may approach and handle people and situations right.* This means learning to use both one's 'head' and 'heart' positively to win the commitment and involvement of people to achieve a common purpose.
>
> Leadership development therefore begins with defining individuals' innate leadership qualities and then enhancing them with the knowledge, skills and self-confidence to be able to apply them effectively. Our courses enable people to *learn from practical experience* which recreates the real and similar problems, pressures and situations that confront us at work. The essential learning comes from the constructive feedback and skilled tuition provided in the reviews after every practical session. The Leadership Trust provides an environment where managers can *practise* leadership, make errors if necessary, gain constructive feedback and learn without threat to their self confidence or career.[54]

The objective of giving people the experience of leadership in a practical way, where there is minimal risk to those being led, is akin to efforts which have been a part of military training for decades. Work in training for leadership, undertaken at the Royal Military Academy, Sandhurst, and the Royal Air Force demonstrates that to improve the effectiveness in any organisation, five areas must be carefully studied. The first of these is the structure of the organisation, which should allow many opportunities for the practice of leadership under varying degrees of supervision. Likewise, a tradition of good leadership should be part of the organisation's value system. Second, formal courses on leadership should be developed to the highest standards. Third, such course work should be tied in with subsequent practical leadership training in the officers' training programme. Fourth, staff members should be given the opportunity continually to study and improve their performance in leadership training. And fifth, a small research and advisory team should be created to maintain and improve standards.[55]

Interestingly, outdoor development programmes give attention to all of these areas in establishing course objectives and in setting objectives for their own staff development. This is one of several areas for reciprocity between outdoor development organisations and management schools. Business schools use the skills of mountain instructors to create experiential learning for their management students. In return, they might offer to the mountain instructors experiences of the business school environment where they may learn more about the theory and practice of management in a classroom situation for their own development and a further enhancement of their dealing with managers on the rockface.

In describing its 'Leadership development programme', the Colorado Outward Bound School says the course is

> . . . offered in the fall and spring with the outdoors as the teaching medium for leadership skills. While the course focuses upon leadership within experiential education, leadership skills taught are applicable to any walk of life. You will participate in teaching, leading, following, project presentation, planning and organizing activities. In the end, you'll develop the knowledge, experience and sense of purpose to act effectively. In addition, you'll learn: general mountaineering, backcountry first aid and emergency procedures, how to deal with wilderness hazards, group dynamics and counselling skills. You'll explore

the moral, social and spiritual dimensions of leadership.[56]

(The objectives are many and perhaps there is more than a touch of oversell in the description, but it does take three-and-a-half months.)

Communication skills workshop

The word 'communication' comes from three Latin words: the preposition, '*cum*' 'with', the word '*unus*' meaning 'one' and a corruption of the verb '*facere*' 'to make'. Thus the complete word means literally 'to make one with.' Not surprisingly, improving communication skills is one of the objectives espoused by most outdoor development training courses. The Brathay Hall Trust, in Ambleside, Cumbria, which runs 'management in action' courses is so committed to the communication objective, that it has a specific drama department which adds this type of communication to the hard tasks of mountaineering and canoeing.

The Leadership Trust, the Outward Bound mountain school (Eskdale) and the South West Regional Management Centre use transactional analysis in their development training. The Leadership Trust employs transactional analysis as an aid 'to self-awareness and self-control, for handling and approaching people and situations properly and to develop leadership skills'. The Outward Bound course employs a TA consultant who helps design the courses and plays a leading role in debriefing the adventure exercises and group dynamics, using transactional analysis. The South West Regional Management Centre uses transactional analysis as a conceptual framework for use by course participants in dealing with leadership experiences.

Dealing with change and uncertainty

The coming shake-up in the industrial world due to the

widespread use of the microprocessor and the impact of new technology will make the role of the manager more critical. The so-called 'third wave'[57] will bring on massive social upheaval as 'things fall apart' and entire new systems of automation and industrial organisation emerge. The manager will have to cope with uncertainty and change on a scale which is unprecedented. To carry people along with him during such dislocations will take leadership, team work and new ways of coping and prevailing in uncertainty.

Finding new ways to develop an understanding of change and skills for coping with uncertainty seems imperative for educators and trainers of tomorrow's managers:

> Much management education has fallen down in failing to relate theory to the hard, practical world of managing resources and people and taking the consequences of decisions. No business game, no simulation, no case-book study can ever approach the reality, because the inevitable emphasis is on the intellectual framework of a problem, and not on living inside a world which contains unpredictable personalities and events, in which the basis of management may change from minute to minute . . . and in which the only thing certain is that nothing is certain[58].

Managers, when placed in the training situation created by an outdoor development programme, are uneasy about the unfamiliar scene. They are not comfortable with projects on the rockface, the assault course or the canoe route. Decisions are called for in a context of great change and uncertainty and the physical and emotional effects of these decisions are felt immediately and at times painfully.

Managers often deal with problems that are known and methods that are well-tried – these present little difficulty. It is when the problems are unknown and the methods are known, or the problems are known and the methods are unknown, or when both the problems and the methods are unknown that the difficulties increase(see Figure 5).

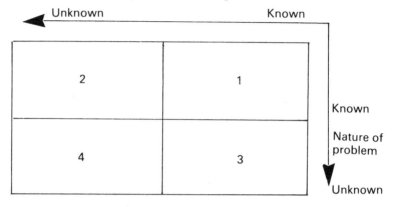

Figure 5   Nature of method of solution

Source: Creswick, C. and Williams, R., *Using the Outdoors for Management Development and Team Building* [21]

Outdoor development is particularly suited for dealing with Box 2 and 4 problems, according to Roy C. Williams, Head of Training and Development for Imperial Tobacco Ltd. Roy Williams[59] summed up the reasons for using outdoor development: it offers reality (no simulation), consequence (not just theory), direct feedback, an opportunity to manage space, distance and time, and genuine engagement in the tasks (the difference between reading a manual on abseiling and doing it). He said his managers found outdoor development courses vivid and memorable, which made the transfer of learning back to the company easier. He had data to demonstrate the high transference. He also found outdoor development highly flexible in design so that he could use it at one end of his company for the board of directors to develop better strategic planning and at the other end for trainees and apprentices to initiate them into management concepts. Ongoing evaluation of the outdoor programmes had made the tailored courses powerful at all levels in the company.

4 DEBRIEFING, EVALUATION, TESTIMONIALS

Securicor does not see these courses simply as outdoor courses. As important as the outdoor elements are: (1) appropriate theoretical inputs by suitably qualified staff (2) the element of stretch – mental and emotional as well as physical – that is built into exercise and projects (3) the constructive and sensitive handling of review (post experience) sessions run by tutors . . . our main reason for using Outdoor Development is that we believe the message is stronger and the effect longer-lasting.

Andrew Brown, National Training Manager,
Securicor

It was the moment of truth. After hours of work, the executive students had finally rigged a ropes-and-pulley system that would carry members of their team across a wide chasm over 100 feet deep. The first man in the queue confided to me nervously, 'I'm so afraid of heights that it took me a week to work up to standing on the top of a

12-foot ladder to paint the ceiling of my lounge'. He leapt off the edge of the ravine into the void. As the harness and pulley took his weight and started to swing him over the waterfall, he amazed everyone by removing one hand from the harness to take a camera from his jacket pocket to photograph the scene below. From the opposite side of the ravine, a TV film crew followed his progress as he was being hauled on to solid ground, a reporter thrust a microphone at him and put the abrasive question: 'Will this help you *manage* better back at work on Monday morning?'

Bordering on parody, the event encapsulates the essence of an outdoor development activity. There was the difficult task on the rockface to be accomplished by team work, imaginative planning and leadership. An element of danger and risk sharpened the moment although, since the activity was carefully supervised by a trained mountain instructor, it was more an illusion of danger than real jeopardy. Fears had to be coped with. Bad judgements and their consequences caused delays and difficulties. Yet a sense of community developed and shared achievement and a certain *joie de vivre* marked the experience. And, after it all, even before the critical debriefing where much learning takes place, there was the intrusion of the outside world in the presence of the film crew to ask nagging questions about the relevance of the experience to the manager's job.

The union film crew from TV (South) repeatedly promised not to interfere with the outdoor development programme underway for part-time MBA students at the Outward Bound school at Eskdale in Cumbria. They then proceeded to want scenes re-enacted, tried (but failed) to get all of the managers from the South racing off together in a Land Rover for a mountain rescue, coopted individual course members and staff with interviews and swamped various activities with a dozen people working energetically. The union film crew came to one debriefing. As the MBA students began to talk about both the physical task – the ravine crossing with ropes and a pulley – and the processes, the three young lady PAs clad in natty French outdoor gear carried their clipboards and scurried noisily about. After two minutes, the producer told the director who told the cameramen and soundmen, 'There's nothing for us here'.

The 28-minute documentary[60] which first went out to the South and then nationwide does, in fact, capture much of the adventure, excitement, fun and even some of the learning which took place on that outdoor development course. But it misses the heart of the matter – the debriefing.

An essential part of outdoor development is the debriefing which is built into each activity. During the debriefing, some of the experiential learning is articulated, peer group evaluations of performance take place and the inputs from the outdoor staff, company trainers or academic staff are made. Discussions during the debriefing often focus on two aspects of the physical activity – task and process – which are separated out to facilitate the analysis. For example, it is helpful when debriefing a 'mountain rescue' activity to distinguish what aspects of the group's performance related to the way they went about the rescue task – responding to the squawking radio and the call for help, organising the stretcher team, orienteering to the place where the injured climber lay, administering first aid and carrying the person back to the base camp. Another discussion would focus on process issues – how the leader emerged (or failed to come forth), how an inventory of expertise in the group was taken, how decisions were made, etc.

Debriefing periods are the best times to draw out the personal, industrial and organisational relevance of the physical experience. In a night exercise, for example, two groups arrived at a small mountain hut in the middle of a forest to find that the hut could accommodate only half their numbers. The first to arrive began preparing a meal with the raw ingredients they found in the hut. Later, the leaders of both groups joined the cooks inside the hut to plan strategy. Meanwhile, the remaining members had no choice but to stay outside standing in a cold, unrelenting rain. As the leaders argued loudly at great length, they never thought to establish a communications link with the troops in the rain whose resentment grew as they remained literally and figuratively in the dark. Reflecting on this experience, one manager said: 'Standing out there in that cold, midnight rain, without anyone telling us what was happening, although we were within earshot of the leaders' meeting, made me feel like shop-floor workers must feel when managers fail to inform them of decisions made around them that directly affect them'.

At debriefing, the essential role of the tutor emerges. Some of the group dynamics and physical tasks can bring out explosive conflict between members of a group. The tutor, charged with maintaining the safety of the group, must be skilful at allowing painful learning to take place without permitting a group to veer on to a destructive course. While conducting their courses, the Leadership Trust keeps an eye open for potential tutors. When they find a manager on the course who controls himself especially well and has the gifts they require in their approach to leadership and team building, they write to his company and invite him to volunteer for training as a tutor. After a day of testing, the selection of the manager as a tutor-trainee is usually confirmed. He then attends two three-day tutors' workshops to learn some basic skills. Next, he is invited to attend an open course as a novice tutor working with a mature tutor. Each year, he is invited to tutors' workshops and asked to do the odd course. The Leadership Trust now has a roster of 180 tutors who augment their 14 full-time staff.

Feedback and evaluation

Most outdoor development courses end on a natural 'high'. It is important when getting feedback that a researcher allows the froth to settle before handing out questionnaires or holding feedback sessions, or at least to have a two-staged evaluation – one immediately after the course and one several weeks or months later.

A typical evaluation of an executive Outward Bound based on questionnaires occurred in October 1977. Forty-four members of the London executive programme (London Business School) out of a class of 58 chose to go on the Outward Bound programme at the Mountain School in Eskdale. They took the train from London to the Lake District and woke to a day of training that seemed more suited to commandos than desk-bound executives. They swung from cables strung from trees 60 feet in the air at high speeds, climbed 14-feet high walls, attacked rope ladders, wire bridges and rockfaces with determination. They leapt from a simulated parachute jump, abseiled a cliff and practised carrying a stretcher down a rockface. They were divided up into four groups of 11 men each and engaged in competitive group dynamics. At night, each group chose a campsite in preparation for an assault on a major peak the following morning.

The small group I was with as a faculty advisor pitched two-man tents above Burnthwaite in the Wasdale Valley. In the morning, with a cold rain falling, we followed a pony track to the corridor route and climbed the Skew Gill. As the cataracts fell around us, we made our way up the slippery rock to the summit of Great End (2,987 feet). We then followed the ridge via Broad Crag and climbed Scafell Pike (the highest peak in England at 3,206 feet) in a hailstorm. At the summit, as we huddled and sheltered behind some huge rocks and ate bread and cheese, a Park Ranger with a dog emerged from the mist and hail to ask what on earth we were doing there in such foul and dangerous weather. It was a question we had all been asking ourselves.

Later, 43 out of the 44 men filled in the three-page questionnaire evaluating the experience. Their ages ranged from 30–50, with an average age of 36½. Of the 43 men, 30 found the course relevant to the London executive programme and 36 felt that the module should be included in the next programme; six said it should not and one man was uncertain. Throughout the questionnaire, they indicated the strengths and weaknesses of the Outward Bound module for managers. One executive student had an extreme reaction against the whole affair. In his evaluation form, he argued that the London Business School, as 'his surrogate employer' was in 'violation of the Health and Safety at Work Act (1974) in its failure to supply details of hazards in advance of requiring such dangerous involvement'. It was a minority opinion of one; in fact, the Business School had arranged for medical examinations for the men beforehand and taken out insurance on their behalf which is standard procedure (see Chapter 5, Risk).

Questionnaires evaluating a five-day course at the same Outward Bound school five years later in the autumn of 1982, for members of a part-time MBA course at the Cranfield School of Management, were very positive about the experience. Twenty-two out of 35 members on the course volunteered to attend. The response rate on the questionnaires was 20 out of 22. All but one of the students found the Outward Bound course 'personally valuable' and everyone felt it should become a regular feature of the MBA course. These management students ranked the stated objectives of the course in terms of which were important to them in the following order:

1   personal audit;
2   communication skills;
3   team building;
4   leadership;
5   confidence building;
6   reassessment of roles; and
7   training potential (for others like their subordinates).

The Cranfield MBA candidates explained the relevance of the Outward Bound course to their managerial activity and to their own interaction as MBA students in an open-ended question. One student said:

> For the first time, we as a group ceased to be analytical observers and became operatives. It thus became possible not only to explore the impact on other people of your decisions, but also to identify

your own reaction to other people's decisions. As this was done in a demanding environment, the decision made had a direct and sometimes painful impact upon you. Hence, it made me realise the extent of the power of the decision maker and how callous he can become if he fails to appreciate the effects his decision will have on the operatives. It 'humanised' the classroom theories.

Another MBA student explained: 'When people are under stress, they react differently than in ordinary circumstances; the course accepts and magnifies these reactions which would develop more slowly in an office environment'.

A testimony in support of the course was made by an MBA student who said:

By appreciating that feelings under the surface may be quite strong and ready to reveal themselves, the course illustrates the need for me to understand that others have different levels of commitment and different perceptions, which may cause interpersonal problems. It helped to underline to me the frustrations of working with others with those different levels of commitment and different perceptions and the need to approach those frustrations more positively and less defensively. The course also raised the problem of competitiveness and the friction this creates between individuals who may have, in the past, been on good terms. There is an obvious trade-off between achievement and anti-social, aggressive/competitive behaviour. This was exaggerated in some instances on the course, but is entirely relevant to a business situation.

In a sentence, another managerial student summed up his experience: 'The important thing in this for me is that I have learned how valuable and essential trust is between the leaders and the followers'.

A year later in September 1983, another group of executive MBA students gave feedback in a similar written questionnaire. They listed in order of priority the *reason* for the five-day outdoor development module:

1 experiential learning/to test theoretical concepts in practice;
2 developing individual leadership skills;
3 group cohesiveness and positive perception of the executive MBA course;
4 developing efficient and effective working teams;
5 to increase personal awareness/character development;
6 to show need for confidence building, planning and the ability to manage in uncertainty.

Among the 'quotable quotes' from the experience were the following:

- 'I can now throw myself off a cliff without worrying about it'.
- 'It increased my confidence in my own ability and in an organised group's ability to meet different, fresh challenges and succeed'.
- 'Vital experience of the causes of organisational cockups in microcosm'.
- 'A learning experience in how to handle unusual situations, how group behaviour differs in practical areas as against classroom discussions – how to look at problems with an open mind as opposed to having fixed ideas'.
- 'It helped self-analysis and clearly demonstrated the vital need to plan and to communicate'.
- 'Strenuous physical exercise takes your mind off sex'.
- 'It'll be alright on the night'.

All outdoor development courses include various physical tasks to be achieved individually and collectively. Not surprisingly the various outdoor organisations have differing approaches to the physical demands of the courses. Most make the physical tasks tough enough to 'stretch' the students and dramatic enough to excite challenge and awaken them without overtaxing their abilities. Many programmes include an 'all night' exercise. This is the most gruelling activity of the course and repeatedly in the evaluation of Cranfield outdoor development courses, the 'night exercise' is singled out as 'the most enjoyable, valuable or rewarding' activity. The Outward Bound school at Eskdale offers a number of 'night exercises', one called 'Muffit', in which the participants impersonate secret agents working with partisans to steal a consignment of plutonium. The exercise involves orienteering in the dark in harsh weather trying to elude the enemy police. In the manner of Le Carré's *Smiley's People,* there are codes and rendezvous in the forest and a deaf mute guide. There can even be humour in the gruelling eight-hour exercise as when a senior executive in a balaclava, while looking for a 'contact', disturbed a courting couple. He rapped on the roof of their car parked in the midnight dark of the forest and put a coded message to the shaken driver, *'Are you the jungle king?'*

An American company, Martin-Marietta Aerospace, created a 'career development course' in collaboration with the Colorado Outward Bound School to help train their managers, technicians and professionals, clerical and support staff. The company hired an outside consultancy firm to do an evaluation of the course. The major finding of the outside consultancy firm was the course's effect on employee turnover. Normal turnover for the company was about 8.4 per cent of the work force per annum. However, for those employees who took both the 'managing personal growth' (MPG) two-day in-company course and the four-day Outward Bound career development course, it was only 1.7 per cent. For employees who have taken the in-company course *only*, the turnover figure is 6 per cent, an improvement over the base-line figure of 8.4 per cent, but falling far short of the 1.7 per cent rate for those who did the in-company course and then went on the Outward Bound module. The consultants sum up their findings by saying:

The impact of the programme on Martin-Marietta

Aerospace Corporation and its employees has been positive. While most of the benefits defy precise quantification, we found increased employee enthusiasm and loyalty, traditional indicators of increased employee productivity.[61]

Myra W. Isenhart attributes much of the success of the Colorado Outward Bound school to the educational methods employed, which are based 'on a learning model which acknowledges that we assimilate and use information which is available in our daily lives, rather than delivered in the classroom. That is, the assumption is that people climbing peaks and running rivers develop insights about leadership, self-reliance, teamwork and risk-taking . . . Learning through an Outward Bound experience is not adding bits of information, but a catalytic process through which the learner integrates his/her experience and interprets them with wider meaning'.[62] The proof of outdoor development lies in the experience of companies and in testimonials from those directly involved in the experience.

One such testimonial comes from David Chambers, Director of the London executive programme at the London Business School where outdoor development has been in use for a decade.

> We spend two and a half days at the Outward Bound mountain school at Eskdale, in the course of our ten-week programme. This means that with travelling, we are away from the London Business School for four days. Until recently we positioned the visit at the end of the first week of the programme, but now we prefer the end of week three or week four.
>
> In answering questions from the group before we go to Eskdale, we are matter-of-fact and fairly offhand. We present it as being fun, as offering novel experiences, as providing an excellent means for removing barriers of shyness or reserve in the group.
>
> We find that before going to Eskdale, lots of participants (probably one third) seriously question why on earth we are going there. After we have been,

there is a staggering unanimity that this has been a really valuable and memorable event, very relevant to jobs and careers.

There are several questions about this experience which I find really interesting, and which I can only answer by hazarding guesses. First, I can see why this is looked back on as a rich and enjoyable experience – but why do we all find it *so* important?

For some of the managers going there even for this short visit, it really does seem to have been an experience in the born-again category. You meet them years later, and it is still the topic most likely to come up in conversation.

I can think of two partial answers, though I'm sure they still leave plenty unexplained.

First, it's very important that each person tackle some *new* activities, that is to say activities new to him or her. For example rope-climbing is new to most of our group, and canoeing in kayaks also. For most of us, it is a long time since we acquired new physical skills and there is a great feeling of extending our scope (as we kept doing when we were adolescent) in doing so. This is also a very useful metaphor for the aims of the academic part of the Programme, where managers are being asked all the time to have a go in disciplines and areas which are new to them.

The other answer came as a surprise to me. It relates to the instructors at the Outward Bound school. These are a very impressive group of people. We all knew that they would possess physical skill and authority. But meeting and working with them, we find that they are people of wide interests and culture, that they are sensitive to the personalities of the individuals in our group, that they can more than hold their own in trading jokes and wordly experiences with a group of witty and worldly managers. To work with these impressive characters, who could obviously make it in the commercial world if they so wished but who have opted for working with (among others) underprivileged teenagers, with very little material reward – this makes a strong impact on a group of people all of whom (including the academics) have opted for a more conventionally secure existence. Dropouts we know about, and they are relatively undisturbing to people in the career system. But these dedicated, hard-working and rather saintly figures do hold up a mirror to us and this is quite a disturbing experience for both the managers and the academics, and at quite deep levels.

So, in summary, it's an experience for our group that I don't fully understand, but I am convinced that it gives us something special and important.[63]

Industry

The Cranfield School of Management uses outdoor development on its executive MBA, the management development programme, the young managers' programme, and the Engineering Industry Training Board (EITB) courses. The Cranfield approach to outdoor development, as evaluated by Charles Rose, one of the executive MBA students, gets full marks. As Mr Rose explains:

The first residential week of the second year of the executive MBA programme was a five-day course at the Outward Bound school, Eskdale, Cumbria. This was a radical deviation from the way the Programme had proceeded until then. The outdoor and physical replaced the intellectual indoor activities.

Twenty-two of the 35 people to start the second year of the Programme attended the course of outdoor pursuits with the following goals:

1   self-development through personal audit;
2   an experience of team building;
3   attitudinal change in the assessment of self and others;
4   the development of leadership;

5 a living workshop in communication skills;
6 an experience of dealing with change and uncertainty.

The students arrived at Eskdale with little or no warning of what was about to happen. They had previously received a kit list and a recommendation that it may be useful to do some running to improve personal fitness.

What followed was for many the highlight of the second year, a series of adventurous pursuits and exercises all designed to facilitate testing exploration and development of the person.

On the first night we had to find camping equipment from a jigsaw of a map and clues – sleep out for the night – followed in the morning, and on subsequent days, by a dip in the freezing tarn, simulated rescue exercises, abseiling, canoeing, mountain climbing, a night exercise, and teamwork tasks.

The participants were exposed to and participated in situations, demands, and tasks which to observer and participant alike superficially bore no relation to the managerial tasks in a modern company. However, when examined, the Outward Bound activities demanded leadership and cooperation in practical ways not previously required on the programme.

An example of the type of task undertaken was a ravine crossing exercise where 11 members had to make a rope bridge and pulley system to transport the group to the other side from available ropes and climbing equipment. Other than having the task explained, the group was on its own to plan and implement their chosen method.

What followed was a process where leadership was transferred to the 'most expert' person who understood ropes and pulleys. Plans of proposed rope and pulley arrangements were made by laying out ropes on the ground outside of the Outward Bound school until one was chosen. Satisfied with the plan, the kit was assembled and transported by minibus to the ravine. At the ravine, the scale of the problem became more real – 100 feet is considerably farther in the mountains than as a diagram on a blackboard.

An advance party of four climbed down the ravine and up the other side, then we threw the line to them again, again, and again! No one could throw 100feet!

It was 45 minutes before a line could be reached by the advance party. The learning in testing all the details of planned operations was complete!

Eventually, the ropes were linked between the sides of the ravine and at last sufficient tension was put upon the ropes to enable the first crossing. All seven eventually crossed the ravine on the rope and pulley system designed and constructed by eleven people more at home in the office than the Outward Bound school!

This brief precis of one of the events in a packed five days attempts to encapsulate the sensation of achievement that accompanied the Outward Bound module of the programme.

An executive on an Outward Bound programme: 'When we left the mountain, it looked unchanged: no difference. None of us could say the same about each other.'

Although the quotation probably overdramatises the experience of Outward Bound, the management student is given the opportunity to use himself, his skills, body, and intellect in a new situation. The learning is about testing his own mental and physical skills to the limit in an environment designed to foster a sense of achievement from successfully completed tasks.

The physical environment is used to stimulate personal risk taking, exposure and the exploration of one's own rules, habits, and constraints. Self-development is seen as the unearthing of personal abilities and capacities which makes the person as manager more autonomous.

One of the interesting features is that power and authority on the side of a mountain comes from different bases than in the work environment. In our mountain rescue exercise, power in the game related to those who had the radios but more importantly the power to organise and lead; leadership was established by a combination of the bid for leadership by the person and the willingness and trust of the group in that person. Leadership roles changed according to the tasks required to be done and the skills available and, unlike the work situation, roles were neither protected nor legitimised by an external power or authority.

Most of the students enjoyed and felt the benefit of the Outward Bound experience. Of the 18 respondents to the post-course questionnaire, 17 said that they found the experience personally valuable, and 18 considered that the most important of the objectives for the module was the personal audit, the self-exploration, and learning.

Much of the learning in the module was about leadership and in considering the transfer of learning to work the Outward Bound module was a success for almost all the participants. Even those who sustained minor injuries considered it a valuable experience.

For a group that went through the two-year part-time MBA process together the Outward Bound module was an experience of living and working together that created a learning environment from which everyone gained: no-one found the experience easy, every participant experienced stress from the interpersonal relationships during the course of the five days and aspects of the course put everyone under pressure.

One of the benefits of the experience was that the students knew more about themselves and their fellows than before and it was found that people generally rated their fellows higher in their estimation than previously.

In assessing the value of the Outward Bound module, it has to be balanced against the other types of tasks that the students undertook on the programme. It was completely different and for most, an experience which had substantial benefits. It felt like a powerful experience for the group but one of the ideas that existed that it would create a divide between those students who went to Eskdale and those who didn't turned out to be completely unfounded. The intensity of the Eskdale experience was shared with the Eskdale staff and the Cranfield faculty and as the group was never together again as a group, it was not transferable to another location which demanded different standards and different tasks.

However, I believe that the success of the Outward Bound module set a precedent for learning for the second year of the programme that the Cranfield School of Management aspects of the programme could not match. The excitement in terms of novel events and experiences compares favourably in most people's view with the relatively academic and more certain existence of the Business School. Perhaps Cranfield was tame after the excitement of Eskdale.[64]

Ian Tanner and Steve Reimann are responsible for outdoor development which began in the spring of 1982 at the Manchester Business School. They described their use of the educational option as 'a collaborative venture between MBS and Brathay Hall Trust.' As they explained, the courses are generally three-and-a-half days' long and are part of the core programme of the executive development programme (EDP) – a 10-week course for senior middle managers; and of the part-time graduate course – a three year part-time masters for young promising managers – and are also being introduced to some of the tailor-made courses organised for specific corporate clients. On the EDP, the outdoor module is held at the end of the third week of the course, and on the part-time graduate course it is held at the end of the first year. They continue:

> The key aim of this course is to provide an opportunity for participants to experience and understand some of the elements that determine group behaviour. Factors such as leadership, communication, trust and team roles are discussed in the review sessions following exercises. A subsidiary aim is to provide opportunities for participants to learn more about themselves at a personal level through participating in the many projects and activities.
>
> To achieve these objectives we create a climate which course members find trusting, supportive,

stimulating and relevant. Much care is therefore taken to set up this environment at the outset.

The three-and-a-half-day programme has been carefully designed to provide a coherent structure. The courses are organised around project groups of usually between 6 and 8 people. Each group has a tutor who is responsible for helping the group to interpret their experiences and define their relevance for their work and personal lives. The first half day deals with familiarisation with the environment and usually includes at least one ice breaking activity. The next two days consist of a variety of projects designed to illustrate different but interconnecting concepts in managerial group behaviour. Typically, the first day will consist of short projects of about one hour. As the course proceeds the projects become longer and more complex. There are also sessions in which participants can acquire skills such as navigation, boat work, and rope work, etc. and activity sessions which allow members to participate in the outdoor activity, usually rock climbing and canoeing. We encourage people to choose activities that they have either not tried before or which represent the greatest personal challenge. The culmination of the course is a 24-hour exercise when the small groups combine to undertake a major project which synthesises the elements of the previous two days.

The partnership with Brathay Hall has been very successful. Over the two years we have combined our respective talents in a most effective way, MBS learning from Brathay about the use of the outdoor environment for personal learning and Brathay learning from MBS about the particular requirements of executive development training. The transfer of skills is such that there is now joint staffing – MBS and Brathay staff splitting tutoring roles as well as logistic functions.

As with the Cranfield School of Management and the London Business School, the Manchester Business School reports a similar and surprising finding! 'The majority of members view the outdoor course as one of the most pertinent and stimulating learning experiences of their programme at MBS'. Quotes from course members include:

- 'I've learnt more about man management in the past three days than I have for the past ten years at work.'
- 'I now realise exactly what organisational climate really means.'
- 'It has been a great opportunity to help me realise what my strengths in a group are'.
- 'It's given me a greater understanding of leadership and more confidence in my own leadership ability.'

and then we hear repeatedly:

- 'It's been really hard work but a marvellous experience'.

Tanner and Reimann, however, admit that not all participants respond positively to this type of outdoor teaching.

There is in the managerial community in general some scepticism about the value of outdoor training and its relevance to managerial work. These attitudes quite naturally find expression in the commitment and behaviour of some of those managers who come on our general management programmes. In some rare instances the programme at Brathay has actually converted people of this view to more open consideration of the value of outdoor work but more generally the resistance to learning which basic scepticism builds up is sufficient to ensure that such people leave this part of our course unwilling to admit that anything substantial had been gained from it. We believe that this is an inevitable result of working with nominated managers who have not opted for this form of learning in the way that some other courses permit. None the less the sceptics have to date been in the minority and we remain convinced that for the great majority of managers attending our general programmes the few days we spend working outdoors at Brathay are a vital element in developing their understanding about the nature of interpersonal relations within working groups. We therefore expect to continue developing this aspect of our teaching activities at the Manchester Business School.

The American experience

Outdoor development in the USA is similar to the British counterpart in terms of the impact on participants. David King and Paul Harmon of Harmon Associates, San Francisco, California describe the effect of the Colorado Outward Bound school's 'career development programs'. This is a four-day course that is run for employees from companies. This particular programme at the Leadville Mountain Centre was attended by 45 participants, mostly from the Martin Marietta Aerospace Corporation. The other participants were from Arthur Young and Company and from the First National Bank in Fort Collins, Colorado.

The outdoor activities included sleeping outside their bunk-house, jogging, rock climbing, which included rappelling (abseiling), games, exercises, ropes course, climbing a 14-foot wall, peak climbs, hiking, map reading, and a 5.3 mile run in under an hour.

The stated goals of the programme were:

1 Identify strengths and weaknesses. Discover greater strengths than anticipated.
2 Clarify personal values through time spent in reflection.
3 Develop communication skills in the context of a small group.
4 Try out some new things.
5 Gain competence in outdoor skills at an introductory level.

Participants reported three major benefits resulting from

the programme: greater self-assurance; a boost in morale; and an enhanced sense of teamwork.

Their comments illustrate these benefits. An engineer commented: 'I take more thought-out risks now'. Another employee said: 'This is a hard place to work and then something like Outward Bound comes along. It shows that this is a people-oriented company'. Another person added: 'Sure the company benefits, you get something like this from the company . . . and you feel like giving it back'.

Reflecting on the teamwork aspect of the course, one young man said: 'It's one thing for me to climb up those rocks; it's another for a middle-aged woman to do it. I grew to respect the courage and strength of people I work with'. Employees often recalled the challenges they faced with other participants in the outdoors and remarked how similar those challenges were to the daily stresses they experienced on their jobs.[66]

More UK evaluation

A selection of comments extracted from delegates' reports on a specially designed field managers' development course run by Andy Neal from APN Development Training gives an inkling of the far ranging personal benefits obtained in outdoor development programmes.

- 'The value of these exercises took an interesting turn during the week as one was able to observe how the stresses, physical and mental, affected each member of the team'.
- 'The course will help me to make better use of available resources and use in-depth planning to achieve business objectives'.
- 'This has been integrated into my own work with good results making me use my time more effectively and profitably'.
- 'It showed the importance of team-work, planning, co-ordination and communication'.

- 'I entered the course with some trepidation but left feeling exhilarated, fulfilled and totally exhausted'.
- 'Being able to learn and be clear through communication'.
- 'In the main, the reaction of physical exhaustion but mental refreshment'.
- 'The personal control I had to exercise in order to achieve common objectives has taught me a lesson as I am rather intolerant'.
- 'It has helped me to think in a more logical manner, which has enhanced my application to the job in that I can plan further ahead'.
- 'The outdoor activities have proved to me that planning and delegation of certain duties are essential if goals are to be achieved'.
- 'No single person, be he insular or gregarious, could fail to benefit from the group activity which was continuous throughout'.
- 'No amount of role-playing exercises could have stimulated so much interest and provided such a realistic situation'.
- 'I would never have thought that a canoe ride would be related to management training, leadership, etc., as it did. I found not only "balance" but patience'.
- 'No right or wrong way of approaching the tasks was expressed. Self development seemed the main objective of the course with my own weaknesses and strengths becoming clearer as the week progressed'.
- 'It is interesting to note that the impression of yourself you feel you are giving to others is not always the impression they receive'.
- 'One can be frank and honest about other members of the team without destroying the spirit of the team'.

Testimonials from senior managers about the Celmi experience of outdoor development emphasise more cohesion in groups.

- 'On return the working group will be more co-operative, communicative and thus more positive and efficient.'
  Andy Todd, senior training manager, Ind Coope

– '. . . a certain bond is established between those who have undergone the experience – in every case an improved relationship.'

Jim Beckford, senior manager, Mars Confectionery

– 'When I tell people what we achieved that weekend, most people's mouths drop open and some flatly refuse to believe it.'

S. Clarke, governor, BBC

– 'For me Celmi was joy, surprise, fun, challenge, good people, superb hospitality.'

Clem Holgate, World vice-president, American Express

– 'A totally positive experience which stimulates mind, body and soul. A unique method of building cohesive working groups.'

Tony Astridge, personnel manager, Berger

Any organisation or consultant in the outdoor development business can reel off the quotable quotes about how right their programmes have been for their clients. It requires a great measure of maturity to admit mistakes that bring 'bad reviews'. It takes honesty to deal openly

5 RISK

On a 100-foot abseil down a rockface in New Mexico, Katherine Slobe, manager of personnel planning and programmes for Xerox, misjudged the position of her feet and let out too much rope. She ended up hanging upside down from the top of the sheer cliff while an instructor told her how to right herself to get out of serious trouble. She surpassed herself and did it. She said of the course: 'It` was a great personal experience. I learned what I always suspected, that you can do a lot more than you think you can if you're willing to try it'.

The first death of a manager on an outdoor development course will put the concept to the test. Companies, business schools and other institutions using the outdoors for management development will have to justify the risks and demonstrate that the learning is powerful enough to absorb an individual personal tragedy.

Despite a tremendous commitment to safety by those who conduct outdoor development and the individual regard to their own safety shown by participants in outdoor programmes, it is not alarmist to predict that the human element and the chance factors of adverse weather may combine to cause serious injury or death to managers climbing a mountain peak, sailing on the open sea or shooting rapids in a white-water canoe exercise. As in industry, accidents happen and are a fact of life.

This is true in the areas of activity which have fed the movement of outdoor development, the military, outdoor sports, Outward Bound, outdoor education and youth activities. During the year of writing this book, deaths have occurred in each of these roots to outdoor development. Two Falklands War veterans died of exposure on a winter training exercise in Norway during the winter of 1983; a world-famous sailor slipped off his boat as it was coming into harbour and drowned; a teacher and his student fell in a rock-climbing accident and were killed; six more rock climbers were killed in Britain during the winter of 1984. Over 42 years of Outward Bound courses in 32 schools in 17 nations, there have been 40 fatalities among the half-million people who have gone on courses; 18 of these occurred in two accidents, one of which was an avalanche. In Britain, there have been six fatalities out of 200,000 people attending Outward Bound courses. There is a tremendous concern for safety in the Outward Bound schools, yet accidents do happen. On a management course at the Outward Bound school in Eskdale, Cumbria, in March 1983, a bank manager fell off a vertical ladder on the ropes course and fractured his back a few feet from where I stood. It was the first serious accident I had witnessed in outdoor development, but it will not be the last and this fact of life must be dealt with in outdoor development.

A full 12 per cent of all companies that responded to my questionnaire, as users of outdoor development programmes, reported having serious injuries. The injuries included two broken legs, a broken ankle, a broken collar bone and one near drowning. This potentially alarming rate of serious injuries must be tempered by two factors. First, certain companies, like GEC, reported no serious injuries from outdoor development activities with a throughput of 2,000 employees per year. Second, there are no collected data on the positive health benefits from outdoor development, which must offset the risks, for example, weight loss of participants due to ongoing commitment to continue regular exercise related to the outdoor experience, or simply giving up smoking because of poor performance in outdoor events. A training manager from Shell said one of his senior managers on the first day of a *conventional* training course died of a massive heart attack while having a bath. Stress and being overweight were believed to have figured largely in his premature death. The experience helped the Shell trainer put potential accidents on outdoor development courses in perspective.

The accidents do not arise from intrinsically dangerous activities such as hang gliding or flying a microlite. It is not a question of risk, as in high-adventure activity such as Himalayan climbing where one out of every ten people has died. It is more a matter of chance accident.

Such accidents can happen anywhere. On a conventional management course in a stately home in the Midlands, the students were asked to congregate in the front garden for a group photograph. The group assembled round a statue of the Goddess Diana mounted on a plinth. Finding himself at the back of the group and unable to see the camera, one of the men put his foot on the base of the plinth and steadied himself by grasping the ankle of the statue. As he did so, the statue fell over and struck him, injuring him.

He sued the management education organisation for negligence and they countered by saying the injury was due to the plaintiff's own negligence.

The particulars of the case look ludicrous with charges that the man 'clambered or heaved upon or endeavoured to mount the Goddess Diana . . . so interfered with or loaded Diana that her mountings broke . . . failed to have regard to the fact that Diana was an ornament'. But the simple fact remains that the man suffered lost-time injury on a routine course and sued.

To protect themselves, both outdoor development organisations and companies or other groups using their services are insured against liability. People attending the courses should have medical examinations; and both the individual and the development staff must have regard for safety.

Outdoor development organisations, in fact, have a strong commitment to safety in all activities. John Sturla, of Haden plc, said his senior managers from the construction industry were impressed by the high concern for safety they experienced on outdoor development courses. He feels that one of the problems of the construction industry is its 'macho' image which he believes contributes to its appalling safety record. The industry attracts 'macho' types and these men cannot appear to be 'chicken' in front of each other, so they do dangerous things. None of that goes on in genuine outdoor development courses, although at times there is competition and peer group pressure to stretch oneself. Business schools, according to Mintzberg, should enhance a manager's entrepreneurial skills by 'designing programmes that encourage sensible risk taking and innovation'. Outdoor development staff maintain that they are providing managers with the experience of risk taking. Testimonials from managers highlight the risk element in the course. Arthur Levitt, Jr, Chairman of the American Stock Exchange, Inc. said:

> Our first confrontation with the rapids was a terrifying experience. But we had our game plan. Each crew had scouted the turbulent waters from the shore and discussed the route they wanted to take. Suddenly we were doing it, flashing by angry looking rocks, manoeuvering our raft by ugly patches of swirling water, paddling furiously first one way then another through the white water turbulence . . .

Mountain instructors and other experts in outdoor sports are always on hand to check and re-check materials and methods. Accordingly, the danger is often more illusory than real. There is no exhibitionism in genuine outdoor development. Fifteen thousand people watched a member of Oxford's Dangerous Sports Club leap from the top of a crane, and hit the ground in a 170-foot plunge at the Pottespury Festival of Transport near Stony Stratford, Buckinghamshire in the summer of 1983. Although he hit the ground at 40 miles per hour, he was, fortunately, not killed. He had just underestimated the amount of elastic rope he needed for the jump. One of his earlier stunts the year before was to ride a grand piano fitted with skis down St Moritz. Any such grandstanding is better left to professional stuntmen, although real lessons can be learned by the person involved. The amateur jumper got his sums wrong despite being a mathematician and using computers to work out the tolerance of his leap.

Adrian Owen, a training manager from the Dewhurst division of Union International, is both philosophical and practical about the risks involved in outdoor development. As a young man he spent four years as an Outward Bound instructor. He developed an instinct for safety which stands him in good stead as a training manager using the out-of-doors. As an Outward Bound instructor he saw a 'competent youth and a very skilled climber' killed when they were swept off a cliff base by a freak wave. They were doing something 'well within their technical competence and the instructor had to make the sort of decision one made every day'. He concluded:

> People often see danger where there are the least dangers. In climbing or abseiling for example, if you've got a guy on a rope you've got him and he can fall but he can't fall far and he can hurt himself but he can't hurt himself badly. He's safe. It's much more dangerous in canoes. If you've got people out in canoes wandering around, which is often seen as a safe and easy option, and the wind can change and boom, you're in trouble; they're off in a dozen different directions.
>
> In fact you look very hard at safety. It's in-built. You're always looking ahead and asking 'what happens if that goes wrong – where's my long stop, where's my catcher?' I don't see a problem with

safety, it simply requires due and proper attention. You go out of your way to make people conscious of safety because you want them to relate it to work as good working practice.

In ten years Union International has had only one serious accident when a course member woke up in the middle of the night, groggy with sleep, and took a wrong turn to the loo, walking straight through a plate glass window. He had cuts, bruises and a broken collar bone. Another participant with brand new, hand-made Spanish boots, felt them shrink on his feet when wet, and cried 'wolf' so often about it, no-one paid attention when he got a nail through one of the boots into his foot and complained about it as they trudged through a forest in the dark.

A group from ICI went to an outdoor development organisation for a weekend course. One of the evening exercises for the ICI men was to rescue 'a princess' who was being held by evil men (the organisation's staff) in a castle. The course delegates unfortunately had too much beer to drink in the early evening and their managers prevailed upon the staff not to cancel the exercise. Eventually, the 'princess' was rescued but two of her defending staff needed treatment in the hospital.

Risk in outdoor development does not only reside in the physical activity but also in the potentially explosive interactions that can take place between participants. During an all-night outdoor exercise a part-time MBA student, who is a British Airways Concorde pilot in real life, decided to lead his small group down through the forest to a road in hope of 'collecting cans of plutonium from the other partisans' in a role play. The pilot first sought clearance for his action from the overall leaders who thought it was premature, but said he could get on with it. He then returned to his small group and urged them to follow him. One member of the group wanted to discuss the matter further before taking action. In the heat of the moment, he struck the Concorde pilot in the groin with a large torch. 'Why did you do that?' the pilot asked in pain. 'To slow you down', he replied. 'You do that again and I'll break your——nose', the pilot said. The dialogue became a choice piece of data for process questions about leadership during the debriefing of the exercise.

In spring 1983, Chris Bonington joined a climb to Scafell Pike with a group of executive students from Cranfield that I was taking through a five-day course at the Outward Bound school at Eskdale. One of his complaints was that we were too shepherded by the Outward Bound staff, so that there was not even the risk of bad map reading which, at that time of the year, would not have posed any real danger, only the grave inconvenience of wandering off for miles in the wrong direction.

It is difficult to balance outdoor development programmes to get the right mix of demanding activity and safety precautions, but trainers seem to be finding the middle ground. Perhaps in the spirit of Sir John Falstaff, discretion should remain the greater part of valour.

6 WOMEN

I learned a lot about myself during the outdoor development course – mainly how far I could cope with mental and, essentially, physical strain. I also learned that I lack the urge to lead, but am a good follower and that I need to improve my communication skills.

Kathy Damouni MBA
Supcon Engineering and Services Ltd

Kathy Damouni, 30, is financial controller of Supcon Engineering and Services Ltd, a construction company based in London, but working throughout the Middle East. She was one woman among 22 men on an outdoor development module as part of an executive MBA course at Cranfield in September 1982. Among the other benefits she cites is a giant step towards overcoming her fear of the dark which hs forced her to leave a light on at night while she sleeps and a renewed commitment to regular sports like running and tennis.

A year-and-a-half after the event, she was full of excitement about the experience which included being the first person in the group to cross a 100-foot chasm on a pulley. For her, the five days were filled with confidence-building exercises. She feels she, and many other managers, could use such a course each year.

She is still keen to conquer a para-zip wire activity that defeated her, when she could not bring herself to step off into space, and had to retrace her steps down from the 40-foot tree platform.

Coping with being the only woman among 22 men, she says, was not difficult. She knew all of them from the MBA course but she was surprised by the way some of the men behaved under pressure and physical strain. Eight of her classmates went up in her estimation during the week, four of them went down in her estimation due to the fact that, in her view, they had the strength and ability to do the exercises but they lacked the will.

'You like people to be successful' she said. 'I can't bear failure – not failing because they couldn't cope, but because they didn't make the effort. People's characters come out in situations like these. You expected your classmates to be supportive as they were on the MBA scene and you were disappointed when under stress they became cruel and selfish'. She chose 'Operation Muffitt', a gruelling eight-hour exercise, as the part of the programme which she found most enjoyable. The course was personally valuable to her because it built confidence; uncovered strengths and weaknesses in herself and in others; strengthened the group's interpersonal relationships; and tested communications skills.

'In normal life we are so cushioned', she said. 'Outdoors you get back to basics; you have to fight for everything'. The confidence-building aspects of the activities helped her to take risks which ran contrary to her 'shy and introverted personality' as she described herself. But there has always been a streak of rebellion in her nature which the outdoor development course stimulated. She went to strict Catholic convent schools in Beirut. Her clashes with authority at school were always mitigated by the fact that she was at the head of her class. She recalls her first financial transactions at age 12 when she was cheated on a foreign exchange deal. In her youthful rebellion she refused to continue on the normal track going to the Jesuit University and opted instead for an American university where as a French-speaking sixteen-year-old she learned English by immersion into class lectures. On graduating among the top five students with a first degree in business administration, Kathy went to work for a construction company, the parent company of the firm she now works for. A few years later the challenge of the job receded and she signalled her intention to leave the company. The managing director was shaken by the announcement and started up a new enterprise to retain her, giving her a dual role in launching and running the new enterprise with him. It provided the fresh challenge she required. She was given the financial control of the new company which specialises in electrical and mechanical engineering in the construction industry.

It is a small company. 'You rarely get the chance to exercise leadership in a small company; it's about team work'. The whole outdoor development exercise in her view focused on team work. At one point when her team was doing very badly on a mountain rescue operation, she assumed leadership and made decisions about what should be done and who should do it. The men listened to her.

Kathy Damouni is not in favour of 'women only' outdoor development courses. It would be an artificial, hot-house environment in her judgement totally unrelated to the male-dominated business world in which she works. Her view of power and influence was in agreement with that of American feminist, Gloria Steinem.

> Women tend to define power differently . . . traditional definitions of power have a lot to do with the ability to dominate other people and benefit unfairly from their work . . . We, as women, on the other hand, tend to define power as the ability to use our own talents and to control our own lives. When we

are tempted to act out power's traditional meaning of dominance, the cultural punishments for such 'unfeminine' behaviour are so great that we tend to pull back, even at our worst, to the use of guilt and quiet manipulation.[67]

Gloria Steinem goes on to make the point that the management style of women tends to be cooperative and collaborative. 'When it comes to content, women's conviction that power has to be earned (especially by women) leads to an emphasis on individual excellence, knowledge and learning'.

Jean Coupe, a self-employed trainer, who used to work with the Community Health Council watch-dogging the National Health Service, attended a five-day course, especially designed for trainers at Eskdale Outward Bound under the direction of a training expert Mary Cox. Jean Coupe was one of two women among fourteen participants on the course, the other being a former outdoor instructor. Although Jean Coupe was not a stranger to hill walking, she was apprehensive about how well she would do on the course. In an attempt to reassure her Mary Cox actually heightened her anxiety with the words: 'Women who do come usually do very well and do better than the men'.

Her moment of truth came during the trapeze activity. She climbed a tall tree to a platform from which she was to spring out and up to catch a trapeze bar. 'I remember being discouraged from the activity because of my height – I'm only five feet tall and the activity was not designed for someone my size. I remember standing on the platform and seeing the faces beneath me looking at me and urging me on saying "Go for it". I suddenly thought "I'd better get this together – O.K. how do you jump?" I said to myself. I concentrated on bending my knees and centred myself right down. Everything around the trapeze went black and the trapeze bar glowed like a red bar. I sprung into the air and got it. The people below me were cheering wildly and I was elated'.

Her standing with the group at first rocketed but the

male dominance of the activities continued. 'When people were choosing a team I was the last person to be chosen', she recalled. 'Once during an all-night exercise, after walking through a bog and up a hill, I got angry at the men and ordered them into a circle. "O.K. we've got to decide" I told them. "You, you and you do this", I directed them as a voice out of the dark which diminished the assertion.

When the men remembered my success on the trapeze they became helpful and then patronising. Jean Coupe has not forgotten the trapeze. It has helped her 'dealing with surgery and radiation' in a bout with cancer. 'I think of the trapeze thing and it reminds me of the resources inside myself' she said.

Brinda Lewry attended the 33rd management development programme – a nine-week course at the Cranfield School of Management, February to April 1981. She was using the course to make a transition at age 56 from her career as a senior lecturer in education at Milton Keynes College of Education to the business world. At the end of the course she set up the Celia Howard Jewellery Design Studio with her daughter, a jewellery designer, which deals in custom-designed jewellery and diamonds.

Brinda Lewry recalled the five-day outdoor development experience at Eskdale Outward Bound as 'the learning experience which stuck in my memory more than anything else' on the MDP course. It has since then served as a boost to her morale as her achievements revealed hidden strengths which were helpful to recall in difficult moments.

She was the oldest participant and only woman among eleven men on the course. She remembers noticing a mistake the leader of the mountain rescue exercise made when he copied down map-reading coordinates that came over a short-wave radio. She saw him transpose two numbers in one of the coordinates and didn't challenge him over it. In the end the mistake was critical and the person to be 'rescued' was not found.

Reflecting on the outdoor development experience three years on she said:

I have never considered myself to be tough, adventurous or physically brave and feel no particular need to prove myself in these respects; nevertheless, I am quite proud of my skills – games and especially dancing.

I heartily dislike groups of women who choose to emphasise ruggedness for its own sake (Guides, hikers, the army, etc.) and show little delicacy but think it useful to cultivate some of the sterner qualities for when they are needed. I quite enjoy competition with men – one can go flat out without actually having to win.

I should have hated going on a women's course (what do they want us to be?) and wonder how they would be constructed. In what ways would women be expected to be different from men. Would the women be treated 'as if' they were men but with modified standards or would it be presentation (playing at nurses instead of soldiers).

Her reservations about a 'women only' course extend to the transfer back to the workplace. 'The more artificial the group the less readily it would transfer to reality'.

In her overall assessment of her performance she said:

I was both amazed and delighted to find I was not the slowest. I carried the same pack as everyone else in spite of weighing so much less. I discovered I have more courage than I had thought although definitely not reckless or foolhardy, and that I do not turn back once committed. That knowledge has been useful to me when making business decisions – it has helped me to rely on my judgement of myself in relation to events. It was also a good opportunity to see how I performed in unfamiliar situations and those in which I do not normally measure myself.

I was interested in the effects of different types of leadership. On the first evening we had to light a fire for tea – everything was soaking wet. One of the men prided himself on his bush craft as he had collected things for firelighting before we went. He sent people to shred minute sticks to get started but they didn't burn. I looked around and brought pine needles (damp but dead) and he said they wouldn't do as they were damp. Having no confidence in green wood, I went to bed. I heard a long time after that it had taken 1½ hours to start the fire and the only thing that would burn was the pine needles! Perhaps I should have asserted myself over the coordinates!

Brinda studied two men on the course with her in terms of leadership style and effectiveness. Her observations are astute.

'Although he was very efficient, I felt leader 'A' saw his group as there to support him – very ego involved. When threatened by failure he became over-anxious and made unreasonable demands, barking even harder up the wrong tree.

Leader 'B' equally determined to be a 'good leader' nevertheless showed a caring attitude, putting his own skills at the group's disposal – encouraging and assisting. He would get mad and lose patience but was always in touch and took on people of his own strength, not weaker ones. He would earn my full support and loyalty.

These experiences led me to think that neurotic drive, while it accomplished much and is highly motivating, can also break down performance if there is not sufficient maturity to recognise and control it. Perhaps I am looking for a sense of proportion and of humour'.

Heather Brundle, a former secretary at a Securicor area office, credits a short outdoor development course at Brathay Hall Trust with giving her the insight into her capabilities that helped her advance to a supervisory position in the company.

She was one of four women among 32 men on the company-run course. 'The course gave me an insight into the kind of people I'm working with in a largely male-dominated company and it gave me a feeling that I could be something more than just a secretary', she said. 'It is difficult to know, as a woman, how you stand in terms of your career development. The Outdoor exercises opened my eyes to my resources and abilities in working under stress and difficult situations'.

She now works as an administrator in the company's national training department with two women reporting to her. Before, as a secretary, she was isolated in an office in Huntingdon near Cambridge. The outdoor experience gave her a different view of the company and its managers. She found Securicor 'more adventurous and go-ahead' than she had thought.

On the course itself, she discovered that she had to be 'quite positive' and 'firm' to get past the natural reluctance male participants had to accepting ideas from a woman. She did not let herself get saddled with the writing or note taking that some of the exercises demanded and that was deferred to her as a woman. 'Throughout the course I had to work harder not just to prove myself as a person, but as a woman.' she said. 'I'm a quiet person and they were surprised at what I had to offer. I got totally involved and I overcame my shyness because I really wanted to make a contribution'.

In her earlier work life she was a scientific government civil servant. Her work included dealings with the British Antarctic team based on her site. But although men and women worked well together on the projects, she found herself doing deadend work, 'boring, dreary, repetitive research work'. She was low in initiative and good at carrying out other people's ideas. There was no future in the field for her as a non-graduate so she left the job and trained as a secretary.

She now has her feet firmly planted on the bottom rung of the management ladder and she has a career path charted. Her memories of how well she had done in orienteering and the boat races are a boost to her motivation.

Louise Roberts has been a senior instructor at Eskdale Outward Bound and a chief instructor at Pacific Crest Outward Bound in America. She has worked as a tutor on many co-ed and women's courses in Britain and the USA. 'In personal development terms I see a need for *both* the co-ed and single sex courses, and do not see the relevance of arguments about which is better, more progressive or retrogressive: both provide valuable learning experiences,' she said, and added:

> The idea of women-only 'managers' courses is interesting but seems largely academic at present; there are so few women on existing managers' courses – in fact men-only is the norm. However, if we look at what happens on a course of 20 managers of whom four are women, we can get some insights into what might be gained or lost in an all-female group tackling the same circumstances.
>
> The tasks set before participants in outdoor development are often technical – requiring a practical rather than intellectual solution. Popular belief has it that women may be academically or intellectually equal, but in technical/ practical matters they don't have the background or the ability to see solutions. Hence you find the women doing the crosswords set by the outdoor developers, finding out who owns the zebra, being consulted for Shakespeare quotes and Latin translations, while the men work out how to get the group over the wall, or build the free-standing structure. If there were only women in the group they would find themselves doing everything, and succeeding with it.

The issues of women's roles in outdoor development should be considered in the context of the goals of the programmes. As Louise Roberts put it:

> Outdoor development courses are also about successful working with team-mates and effective leadership. Often a woman trying to take the initiative in a practical exercise (unless it's First Aid) will not be welcomed by her team-mates and may experience antagonism or, more frustrating, indifference and dismissal. (Aware of all this a woman may put forward her solution through a powerful male member, and

be indirectly influential in the successful conclusion without recognition. Many women find such games necessary at times.)

This has significant implications when looked at in the light of the hopes, expectations and aims of the course. One of the themes of outdoor development exercises is the taking of risks, social and emotional as well as physical, as a growth process and learning experience. This involves sticking one's neck out and taking responsibility for part of your group's plan, tying one of the knots you're all going to trust, making a crucial map reading decision at dead of night, offering your shoulder for someone's feet to surmount an obstacle: taking responsibility for planning a task, putting it into practice and completing it, being involved in it from start to finish, making it *your own* by so doing. Something vivid and real. Experiential education at its best.

My fear is that women (and men) who allow themselves always to be led, to be helped over every stile, to be pushed out of the way on the construction site, etc., are missing out and selling themselves short. Their gains in personal growth are diminished. If this happens to women in an all-women group it perhaps tells them more about themselves than if it is their behaviour in a mixed group.

In mixed groups a much more definite step is needed to break away from traditional or assumed roles, and in outdoor situations which are new and somewhat threatening to all participants people tend to fall back on secure and familiar relationships, rather than going out on another limb – the abyss looms all too deep as it is. Thus men who are apprehensive but unwilling to express their apprehension will encourage women to emphasise and show their fear, by adopting sympathetic and protective roles. Certain characteristics are expected of men, others of women. This inhibits the expression of so-called male traits in women and female traits in men. It is still very common for people on management courses to be role-bound, despite much written and verbal knowledge of it.

To sum up her views Louise Roberts said: 'Perhaps our paramount need is an adventurous approach to role experimentation on outdoor development courses, to free all of us in our interpersonal relationships, rather than gaining our freedom by the elimination, either physically or psychologically, of the other sex.'

Conclusion

The 'macho' image of the activities and the disproportionately low number of women managers tends to keep women's participation in outdoor development low. This is particularly unfortunate in the light of government efforts to diminish sex discrimination. The Sex Discrimination Act 1975 does not permit 'reverse discrimination' whereby an employer would discriminate *in favour* of women in recruitment or promotion out of motives of restoring the balance or allowing women who have suffered from job discrimination in the past to 'catch up'. Such action would be unlawful. However, the Act does permit certain forms of 'positive action',[68] or what the Americans call 'affirmative action', and these are all in the training area. The training organisations which may take advantage of the provisions of the Act permitting 'positive action' are:

Manpower Services Commission
Training Services Agency
Employment Service Agency
Industrial Training Boards
Those bodies specifically designated for the purpose by an order of the Secretary of State.

These training organisations can exercise 'positive action', for example, when it appears to them that during the previous twelve months there were no women engaged in particular work or that the number of women engaged in such work was comparatively small. Likewise if during the course of a year no women or relatively few women took the test for particular work, a training organisation could offer special access to training programmes to women as a form of positive action. Married women who have given up work to bring up a family and later wish to return are also eligible for 'positive action' training programmes.

Employers themselves can provide special training for women only if the particular work is either done exclusively by men or largely by men. Similarly trade unions, as employers, and employers' organisations and professional bodies, may take 'positive action' to ensure that members of both sexes are fully represented at various levels in the organisation.

In any form of 'positive action' training for women there is scope for outdoor development as part of the discriminatory package. Women benefiting from such 'positive action' could attend special outdoor development courses designed for their particular training needs on a women only basis or better they could attend open courses relevant to their training needs where there would be both women and men participants.

Some would argue that the lack of greater numbers of women in attendance on outdoor development courses simply mirrors the disproportionately smaller numbers of women in managerial positions in industry and commerce. But there is no reason why outdoor development programmes could not be incorporated in efforts in an affirmative action approach to this glaring sexual inequality. As a slogan of the 1960s put it: if you're not part of the solution, you're part of the problem.

7   CONCLUSION

The acceptance by companies regarding the value of outdoor development training will not be accomplished overnight. The objective must be a long-term one of spreading the gospel amongst our younger managers and employees.

D. Webb, GEC

Evaluating outdoor development is a research task for the future. Elliott[69] believes that the evaluation of the effectiveness of outdoor management training involves answering four major questions; what, by whom, when and how.

What involves a consideration of the objectives of outdoor management training. These objectives can be considered in a hierarchy from the vague and general (to develop better managers) to the specific and measurable (to improve objective setting). Objectives should be specified in behavioural terms.[70]

By whom refers to the fact that we could be assessing the objectives of the course from the viewpoint of:

- the participant;
- the course director; and
- the participant's manager.[71]

When to assess involves a consideration of:

- immediate;
- intermediate; and
- ultimate objectives.

How to assess can only follow from a consideration of the first three questions since the variables being measured have to flow from a consideration of the objectives. Some suggested methods of assessment are:

1 the repertory grid, using various different types of elements;
2 standard questionnaires (for example, a situational sensitivity scale);[72]
3 projective instruments, such as self in the organisation, managerial projective tests or case studies used in a projective way;
4 open-ended self-descriptions leading to content analysis; and
5 structured self-description, using, for example, an adjective checklist.

Many techniques can be used singly or in combination. Elliott feels that extensive interviewing of participants, directors and managers would be a useful first step to help us decide the appropriate type of instrument and the questions or elements to be used.

Alan Mossman[73] acknowledges the difficulty of the review and evaluation of the effects of outdoor management development: 'The nature of the learning that participants and trainers describe make it difficult to collect in conventional questionnaires . . . . it seems to involve learning how to learn.'

He recommends administering the repertory grid (Kelly's

grid) to people before and after the outdoor development experience. He also recommends participant
observations to help link up the physical activities with the
individual's learning. He argues that an evaluation of the
outdoor development programme in isolation would not
be satisfactory because it should be compared with its
alternative – a 'conventional' management course. This
would require comparison of data from four discrete
groups of managers:

1   those who experienced outdoor development;
2   those who took 'conventional' short courses;
3   those who were subject to the same level of atten-
    tion as the two previous groups but took no
    courses; and
4   those who received neither course nor attention.

Another whole area of research would focus on the
outdoor development organisation to analyse their
motivation for the work, their pedagogies, the competence of their staff in working with managers and their
ability to build bridges back to work.

On a very basic level, the amount of company interest
and involvement in the area needs to be mapped. The
questionnaire reproduced in the Appendix could be
targeted to companies with whom the reader has a special
working relationship to facilitate our collection of data at
Cranfield.

It should be clear from the collective experiences of
thousands that there are real and lasting benefits for
managers which derive from outdoor development,
however difficult it is to quantify or measure them. Surely
a strategy for management development which makes as
many claims as outdoor development does cannot be
dismissed out of hand. Any strategy with potential to
improve the performance of managers at many levels in
organisations is worthy of a full and rigorous investigation.

Difficulties over a scientific evaluation of Outdoor
Development are not surprising. The problems of
evaluation research seem to be much the same in

education, industry, the army, the church, marketing and politics. 'Evaluators in these fields seem to encounter the same obstacles, such as the innumerable variables, the vagueness of objectives, opportunistic or intuitive decision making, the element of change and freedom of action, the unreliability of measurements and the reluctance to believe that any assessment of the effectiveness of programmes is possible.'[74]

Evaluation research can be defined as a 'scientific assessment of changes in human behaviour as the result of influencing methods and as a factor in the process of change'. In the light of the principles of genuine evaluation research, Outdoor Development may raise a false dilemma. The researcher, on the one hand, must include the *subjective* element of human experience in evaluating an Outdoor Development programme especially if he has been involved in the action itself and when he therefore must struggle with inadequate data coming from many 'contaminated' sources. It is difficult not to show a built-in bias in such circumstances, particularly if the researcher is himself a 'true believer' in using the outdoors for development. On the other hand the researcher, to be faithful to his research task, must try to design an *objective* system of tested formulations to determine the effectiveness of action programmes such as Outdoor Development. In academic jargon this involves a systematic rotation of dependent and independent variables. Perhaps two extreme and contrasting views on this dilemma will illustrate the conflict.

The first would emphasise the *uniqueness* of the process of change and specific situation arising for example from an Outdoor Development intervention in a company. Since the training objectives and the value orientation of those doing the training and those experiencing the training are different in every different situation, the uniqueness of each process becomes paramount. Training is viewed as an art based on an intuitive grasp of the specific situation which itself fluctuates. Hence any attempt to structure the subtle feedback between trainer and the training situation and to calculate individual personal reactions, is a distortion of the reality. There can be no measurement. The only possibility for improvement lies in the development of an increased sensitivity in relating to interpersonal reactions.

The second view – diametrically opposed to the first – would stress the need to impose strict rules for the optimal pattern of action programmes and have perfect scientific instruments to control the change process. They would create a master plan which would embrace the human, technological, political, cultural and economic variables over a long period of time and be based on an integrated forecast of the possible outcomes.

Both views are wrong. To say that the results of a training intervention like Outdoor Development cannot be measured is just as erroneous as to say that the measurements must be perfectly accurate and comprehensive. At the outset a researcher should admit the limitations of his trade. He simply does not have the instruments and methods to measure the results of the complex learning process. The knowledge, attitudes and skills that are the components of any training intervention cannot easily be related to the changing environment, particularly as people have different value orientations.

Imperfect measurements are nevertheless important. It would be wrong for the researcher to throw up his hands and despair of evaluating something as complex as an Outdoor Development programme. Simple, crude and even inaccurate measurements can provide insights into complex relations which stimulate fresh development of the training process. Data-based knowledge of the objectives, the process and some effects of the training intervention called Outdoor Development in specific situations has two spin-offs.

1 It helps to improve the Outdoor Development programme
2 It fosters an understanding of the change process.

A study[75] conducted ten years ago of British character-building Outdoor Development programmes concluded that: 'although the characters of trainees may be modified, their behaviour and attitudes at work and leisure are more rarely affected (by Outdoor Development). The courses' effects upon trainees' characters can ripple outwards to influence their social behaviour, but there are few indications of the main types of social change that organisers and sponsors seek'.

The longer-term effects of the courses, the researchers claimed, were found mainly 'within the personalities of the trainees'. Following their training most young people were found to feel 'different', more mature, self-confident, and better capable of handling relationships with others. The researchers then add: 'However, organisers and sponsors do not support courses merely to give youngsters' egos a psychological boost; they are looking for a social spin-off, and here the sum of the evidence now points in a negative direction'.

This judgement is immediately qualified: 'the conclusion that the wider social effects of courses are slight must be tempered by the complexity of the problem under discussion. Courses' effects may vary along with the nature of the training, the initial dispositions of trainees and the environment to which they subsequently return ... Having demonstrated that such variations occur we must qualify our conclusions ... we must ask whether the absence of marked changes in the social lives of the greater number of the trainees we studied could have been due to the peculiarities in the firms upon which our investigations were based. In the companies studied, although often tending to be 'better' employees, the youngsters sent for training were not all destined for promotion, courses were not carefully integrated within longer-term and progressive programmes of training, no real attempts were made to follow-up the courses nor to match individuals' needs to particular schemes.'

If the researchers found the youth end of the Outdoor Development market difficult to deal with in terms of formal evaluation of effective training, it is not surprising that evaluative research of Outdoor Development for mature managers remains in its beginning and tentative stages. Researchers, course participants, companies and

Outdoor Development organisations should all co-operate in the challenge of evaluative research, for the payoffs could be as numerous as the difficulties.

Early in 1962, President John F. Kennedy gave an executive order in writing to have US missiles removed from their silos in Turkey. His decision was made after examining alternative strategies and the recommendations of the Joint Chiefs of Staff, the State Department and the National Security Council. Several months later, at the height of the Cuban missile crisis, President Kennedy was amazed to learn that his order had not been carried out and that his control system failed to report this breakdown in his executive authority.[74]

From presidents to heads of multinationals to middle and frontline managers, the manager's job remains a complex one which intermingles interpersonal, informational and decision-making roles. Research reveals that the manager in action is far from the classic model of a person who plans, organises, coordinates and controls. The pace and pressures of his position, as Mintzberg points out:

> drive the manager to be superficial in his actions – to overload himself with work, encourage interruption, respond quickly to every stimulus, seek the tangible and avoid the abstract, make decisions in small increments, and do everything abruptly.[75]

The multiplicity of the manager's roles requires skills as well as knowledge. Hence, it is the task of management development to attempt to inculcate in its students skills as well as cognitive learning. Yet while lectures and books can be used to transmit knowledge, skills can only be learned by practice with feedback from tutors and fellow students, and perhaps video cameras. The catalogue of requisite skills for managers includes the skills of negotiation and communication, of motivating others, of handling conflicts, of networking and channelling information, of coping with uncertainty and ambiguity, of decision making and of dealing with totally new situations. It has been the main argument of this book that outdoor development has a powerful contribution to make towards the making of a real-world manager.

Management as an institution will not vanish from future society. It will prove indispensable and management development will continue to have a vital role in the new millennium. The most successful companies have a strong commitment to developing their managers and this will increase. IBM, for example, spent more than $500 million (US) on employee education and training in 1982. In the same year, the company had profits of $4.4 billion on sales of $34.4 billion, making it America's most profitable industrial company.

Experts tell us that managing under attack and in uncertainty will rapidly become the norm in the turbulent years ahead. They forecast upheaval and changes in the form which management takes in terms of restraints, controls, power, structure, and rhetoric.[76]

In such a challenging environment, the manager will continue to be, in Drucker's words, 'the dynamic, life-giving element in every business', and he will rightly expect those who claim to teach and to train him to use a dynamic and life-giving pedagogy.

Can outdoor development meet this demand? In its early days outdoor development holds up to the manager the promise of widening his experiential knowledge, fostering attitudinal change and helping to develop the practical skills he needs to face a future of uncertainty and ambiguity.

But can outdoor development deliver in the long term? Does it have staying power?

The future is a testing ground for managers where challenge will be inescapable. Managers who take up the challenge will discover personal relevance in the Outward Bound motto: 'to serve, to strive and not to yield.'

PART II
OUTDOOR DEVELOPMENT IN ACTION

CASES FROM COMPANIES

The particular course that we run combines assessment centre techniques with outdoor training. It is aimed strongly at developing individual young managers. Due to the excellent results that have been achieved it is planned to open the course to higher level managers. An increasing interest is being shown in using the outdoors for team-building and development.

A.F. Hands, Cadbury-Schweppes PLC

In May 1983, with the help of Hugh Butland, an MBA student at Cranfield, I sent out a questionnaire on the use of outdoor development programmes to nearly 900 of the *Times'* top 1,000 companies in Britain (see Appendix).

Within two months, 16 per cent of the companies responded, which is a good response rate to a cold mail shot. (The norm is 10–15 per cent for an initial shot to a named mailing list.) Of the 140 respondents, 32 per cent already used outdoor development, 59 per cent wanted to discuss the topic and a full 78 per cent requested a copy of the research findings. The conclusions are promising for the future of outdoor development.

The biggest users are GEC, Securicor and Safeway whose programmes will be described later in this chapter.

Personal development was identified as the principal benefit to the companies that use outdoor training programmes. Team building and leadership were also ranked high. Most companies found it difficult to specify immediate tangible benefits, although one company reported increased profitability from using outdoor development. Interestingly, the GEC and Securicor ranked the benefits of outdoor development identically as follows: personal development, communications workshop, team development, leadership development, and managing in uncertainty.

- The Leadership Trust, Outward Bound, Brathay Hall and in-house courses topped the list as the most frequently used organisation.

- Rock climbing and canoeing were the most frequently used physical activities among the many mentioned.

- The majority of the companies use formal evaluation of the programmes and the services of a company trainer, but 'organised reviews' were mentioned only four times.

- The rate of serious accidents was high for the response numbers – three serious leg injuries, one broken collar bone and one near-drowning.

- Most companies heard about the topic from outdoor development organisations marketing their courses.

The most often cited reason for *not* using outdoor development courses were:

1   too expensive
2   not proven

3 short on theory
4 benefits and relevance unclear
5 too busy with business.

Companies that do not currently use outdoor development would try it for the following reasons:

1 if it had senior management's approval
2 when the company recovered economically
3 when the training budget was increased
4 if its potential worth were proven
5 if it added a dimension to the existing management programme
6 if well-organised and well-validated outdoor programmes were made available commercially
7 if it were demonstrated to be cost-effective compared with other action-based learning vehicles in use.

Two comments that may well be signposts for the future of outdoor development were:

1 Outdoor development seems a systematic next step in our management development programme.
2 We might consider using outdoor development when some research has been completed which identifies and quantifies the benefits offered and gained by this type of programme.

The 10 cases that follow are indicative of the range of industries that have found outdoor development useful for their managers. They also provide an interesting assortment of goals for embarking on outdoor training programmes with notable outcomes.

1 American Medical International (AMI)

Throughout the world, AMI owns over 100 hospitals and health centres. They are concentrated largely in the USA. In Britain, AMI owns ten hospitals. It has been operating in the UK for only ten years. During such a brief span of time and rapid expansion in the UK, AMI has not been able to produce its own managers and staff; many have been taken from the National Health Service. Others came from the hotel and catering industry and from the military services. This has made for a disparate group. Coming from the public service sector by and large, they had first to develop a commercial attitude to their work as well as a professional and caring attitude. This required adjustment.

The changes and the speed of growth in the young company also created uncertainty and insecurity among the managers, especially those from the National Health Service who were not used to changes. But the most difficult problem the management teams faced was not their adjustment to a commercial operation or dealing with a disparate team, or even coping with change, it was something to do with the way hospitals were set up.

The management team is headed by the hospital director, who has a managing director's role. Beneath him are the department managers. They come on site many months before the hospital receives its first patient, to commission the hospital. Together they set up systems, get the physical plant ready, bring in the equipment, hire and train the staff, etc. Commissioning a hospital is a one-off crisis management situation. Once the hospital is open, the management team must move from the commissioning mode to the operational mode. Within six months to a year, AMI found that some of the management team became bored with the operational aspects of running a hospital after the excitement of the commissioning phase. Moreover, those members of the management team who did the commissioning had formed a tight team. As new people were brought in to the hospital and as some of the original team were promoted to other positions or left, their replacements, or the new people added to the team, remained an 'outsider' group compared with the 'insiders' who had set up the hospital.

Traditional management development training was not able to deal with this specific problem. It did not get down to fundamental attitudes or change behaviour. It did not break down the old *vs* new team situation.

The Priory Hospital in Birmingham provided the first opportunity to deal directly with the specific problem. Its situation typified the old/new team problem. In fact, the director, David Prattent, was a 'new' person who had not been there during the commissioning and found himself on the outside trying to get in. It was his idea to take the entire hospital management team to the Outward Bound mountain school in Eskdale for a short outdoor development programme. The management team included the hospital director and deputy director, the director of nursing, one senior nursing administrator and department managers for the various functions – catering, domestic services, pharmacy, radiology and pathology, laboratory, physiotherapy, X-ray and hospital engineering, and the materials manager and business office manager.

The outdoor development programme dissolved the differences between the group in terms of those who had taken part in the commissioning and those who arrived at the hospital later. The shared learning experience in the outdoors created a team from people of many different disciplines, backgrounds and classes. It has given AMI a training model to work to for all of their hospitals here and a management development programme to export to AMI health care centres worldwide.

2   Provident Mutual Life Assurance Association

Provident Mutual has about 1,000 employees (300 sales staff and 700 administrative staff) scattered over 24 branches throughout the country with £1,350 million in funds. Since the early 1970s, the company has been using outdoor development. The introduction of the idea came from the chief executive, Brian Richardson, CBIM. Nine years ago when he became director and general manager of the company, he put together a senior management team and began instilling principles of leadership at lower levels in the company. He felt that members of middle management in the company tended to develop 'coursemanship' to deal with traditional management education. They knew what was expected of them in the classroom. To break the mould, Mr Richardson turned to the Leadership Trust and to Brathay Hall Trust to focus on outdoor leadership training for his middle managers and for junior managers who were A level and graduate intake.

The outdoor development is integrated fully with an employee's overall management development. Junior managers start off with a 14-day Brathay Hall Trust course, focused on leadership and personal skills. By the time they are ready for their first middle management course, they are sent on a five-day Leadership Trust course which gives them the practice and experience of leading groups in the testing outdoor environment. 'On the outdoor programme, no-one can hide his managerial weaknesses behind a mastery of technology, which is easily done in my industry', Mr Richardson said. 'The outdoor aspect tends to strip a person naked of his trappings of status in his organisation and in his personal life. He must rely on his own skills'.[77]

There is less of a re-entry problem for the manager who returns from an outdoor development programme on a 'high' and wants to implement what he has learned immediately because over the years many managers have been through the courses. Mr Richardson summed it up: 'The general philosophy taught on these leadership courses surfaces in day-to-day practice and our approach to problem solving at Provident Mutual'.

3   Dunlop Limited

Dunlop is a diverse multinational with a range of products from tyres for the family car to brakes and wheels for the new Boeing 757s, from sports gear to industrial and engineering products. Yet its most famous product is tyres and there has been a sharp decline in the tyre market worldwide which has adversely affected the UK operation. Over the last five years, as a result of restructuring and rationalisation in the UK, employment has fallen by

23,000, halving the work force. This has created a climate of insecurity and great change within the firm.

'The accelerating rate of change throughout the economy is apparent for all to see and a constructive approach to identifying and developing the talents of the new generation of managers is a key element for business survival and new growth', was how John Cole, senior training advisor, summed up his company's need.[78] Mr Cole was one of the originators of Dunlop's personal development and leadership programmes (PDLP) which, remarkably, combine training and assessment in the same programme.

The personal development and leadership programme has been developed over the last three years. It takes the manager to the Outward Bound School at Aberdovey in Wales for the total learning experience. Both outdoor exercises and the assessment of management skills, using indoor exercise and personal insight, take place at the Outward Bound School. Questionnaires, interviews and counselling are used to gather and process personal data for assessment.

The delegates were between the ages of 24 and 35 and had been singled out by their supervisors as having potential for moving into first-level management or specialist positions.

The objectives of the PDLP were to develop leadership and team membership, initiative, interpersonal skills and self-confidence, whilst identifying personal development needs and career potential. (The structure of the course can be seen from Figure 6.)

As the figure illustrates, outdoor team tasks, individual insight techniques and indoor exercises are combined to try to increase the young manager's effectiveness in his current job with a view to his next stage. The development focuses on him as an individual, a manager of resources and a team member.

Mr Cole explained the insight techniques part of the course.

These generate information by the participants about themselves and others. Reference has already been

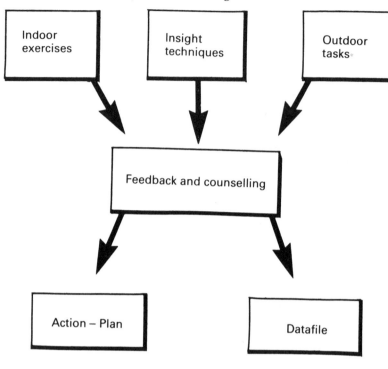

Figure 6   Course structure

made to insights that may be derived from the exercises, particularly interview and Management Evaluation. Perceptive Thinking exercise is likely to raise additional self-viewed operational and psychological characteristics.

Questionnaires and inventories result in own profiles of team roles, personality, learning styles and current job from the job-holder's viewpoint.. Perceptions of each member by the others within his team are built up in descriptive and in quantitative terms. Rankings are obtained on five separate dimensions and they take place as the final scheduled activity of the residential week. This is the only occasion in the whole Programme when sources are not retained and revealed.[79]

During the week at the Outward Bound school, a file is built up on each individual which contains all written exercises and assessment forms for the exercises. Tutors for the programme use the file for about a two-hour feedback and counselling session which takes place several weeks after the residential course. The two-stage session is frank. During the first stage, the manager is taken through the file in detail by the tutor. He is told to develop a strategy to use his strengths, work on his weaknesses and modify his behaviour. He has the right to veto any item that emerges in the session.

Phase two of the feedback takes place at another meeting with the manager's boss who has been briefed on the goals and methods of the PDLP beforehand. The tutor leads the manager and his boss through the file and a discussion ensues on how this assessment of the candidate's strengths and weaknesses compares with his performance on the job. The end product is an action plan for the manager.

After six programmes with about 100 management students in all, Dunlop makes the surprising data-based claim that in formal evaluations of the programme there is virtually no objection from the delegates to the combination of development training and assessment. The benefits they list include:

1 Senior managers report favourable changes by the delegates in terms of behaviour, attitudes and motivation. They have also benefited from being put in touch with their subordinate's aspirations and his strengths, weaknesses and potential.
2 The open discussion has stimulated continuing performance review and career planning.
3 Managers know more about themselves and their roles as leaders and team builders. They also have more confidence and a greater appetite for responsibility and challenge.

4   Plessey Telecommunications Limited

Plessey has two major businesses – telecommunications and electronic systems. From 1978 to 1982, the company nearly tripled its profits to £111.4 million. At the same time, sales rose from £611 million to £963 million.

Telecommunications, with 14,000 employees on 10 sites, represents 40 per cent of the group's sales and 55 per cent of its profits. Plessey has been a leading force in information technology. It has great experience in solid-state-micro-electronic technology needed for large telecommunications and electronics.

The assumptions behind Plessey's commitment to management development include:

1   the best method of development is self-development;
2   learning and personal growth are most likely to take place through actual work experience;
3   management skills are developed by responding to real problems of increasing difficulty;
4   experience should be planned to maximise opportunities for learning; and
5   learning can be accelerated by providing programmes of work-related projects and assignments.

The problem with this classic approach to management development is that it is limited to a very small number of people – in Plessey about 30 people out of 35,000. The idea of incorporating outdoor development into the management development programme was to make development training available to employees other than the 'high-flyers'.

According to Michael Horgan, management development and resourcing executive: 'Properly designed outdoor development has a significant and most importantly lasting effect upon the people who are involved'.[80]

Plessey uses outdoor development at three levels for apprentices, graduates and middle managers. At the apprentice level, where Plessey's use of outdoor development began five years ago, the emphasis for the 18–20-

year-olds is on self-development and achievement. The week-long programme for the graduates is similar with the focus on leadership and self-development. It comes after three years with the company as part of a five-week management course which is spread over the year.

The managers' course emphasises skills of review, assessment and observation, while the apprentices' and graduates' courses are conducted at Outward Bound, Eskdale, the middle managers' course is run at Brathay Hall Trust.

The advantages of outdoor development for Plessey are:

1　leadership and interpersonal skills are brought into clear focus (especially in an industry where technological competence is king);
2　lessons are learned, not taught. *Telling* people to change has only a short-term effect, experience is crucial;
3　theory is kept to an acceptable minimum (the principles of action-centred leadership are used);
4　physical stress and potential danger sharpen up problem solving and decision making;
5　working effectively in groups becomes a functional necessity not just a pleasant social activity;
6　behavioural changes help change attitudes; and
7　there is an appeal to the whole man, to his skills, his courage and his need for action.

Unlike Dunlop, Plessey does not gather quantitative data or have extensive follow-up activity, although the employees are encouraged to develop action plans before they leave the course. After nine months, they return to the outdoor development place for a refresher weekend. Mike Horgan finds that the outdoor courses contribute to making Plessey's engineers less task-oriented and more people-focused. It teaches them to delegate and to make decisions in circumstances of increasing change, which happens to be the environment in which Plessey Telecommunications not only survives but prevails.

5   Unigate Dairy Holdings Limited

The Dairy company is an embattled sector of Unigate, a broadly-based consumer and industrial service group. In its UK milk operations, it must deal with political and regulation problems and a steady decline of doorstep sales.

As weight-conscious people steer away from milk and dairy products and economy-minded families feel the effects of the recession, the market continues to shrink. The controversy concerning long-life French milk is an example of the adverse market forces which further threaten Unigate's dairy market.

The motivation of Don Reeves, the company's personnel director, for going into outdoor development was to help his managers deal with decline. He cites over-manning, declining sales at 2.5 per cent per annum, the effects of recession, bogus pay and reward systems due to incomes policies, and the unique, entrepreneurial custom and practices of milk roundsmen as contributors to the current business reversal. He recognised a need for his men to manage change and decline.

He claims that his business has had more change inflicted on it in the last five years than in the previous 50. No one had been made redundant before and the traditions were very strong and stable.

Don Reeves chose Challenge Training as the outdoor development organisation to meet his objectives, 'to hammer them mentally, physically, and emotionally', to get them to manage change better. He has a flair for the imaginative physical tasks. He asked his managers, for example, to construct a raft out of materials to be able to take a cargo – military textbook stuff – and then the cargo is revealed to be a live goat or three geese which they must first catch in a field. In another exercise, the men discover a luggage locker key and must decide where it is from and what to do about it in relationship to the objectives of the exercise.

He wants them to discover if they can lead, take part in a team, stretch themselves. The oldest manager he had on the course was 61 and 'came out shining'. He feels it is important for senior managers to go on the outdoor course and advised them to do it at the beginning of the course, before the younger managers return with misrepresentative 'macho stories'.

He also recommends that personnel managers and trainers go on outdoor courses themselves, to understand them personally before putting their managers through it.

Don Reeves films as much of the outdoor action as possible with a fish-eye lens. Three months after the event, he has a review and shows an edited version of the film. With the powerful video evidence, the course is revived and the lessons are deeply pondered. It is then that targets for each manager are jointly set to help them strengthen weaknesses, and to manage better in uncertainty, or, as their milk marketing jingo has it, with more 'bottle'.

6 Haden plc

Haden is part of a worldwide engineering firm whose British operation with 20 branches nationwide is the largest in the construction engineering services field. Turnover in 1982 was £283 million and gross profits were £8.6 million.

At first thought, a construction company would be a most unlikely advocate of outdoor development. If this type of management development did little more than provide hairy-chested 'macho' outdoor activities, it would be quite superfluous to a construction firm where normal work life is outdoors and the accident rate is among the highest in the country.

Haden's group training manager, John Sturla, has come on to outdoor development as part of an effort to develop managers at Haden. His action is proactive, as his training department foresees role changes for the managers in the middle term. They were picking up three signals:

1   branch managers are going to become proprietors

with less domination from head office – less reporting;

2   project management is at a crossroads. Pareto analysis was already applied to systems and procedures, to get them right. The question mark is over where improved performance will come from; and

3   greater emphasis will be put on sales management.

Several characteristics of the project environment made it particularly conducive to outdoor development training. Projects are extremely goal-oriented temporarily. They are also in constant change and have distinctive life cycles. To make matters more difficult, they have a good deal of both organisational conflict and personal conflict. Past training did not address these problems and they did not know what to do until they stumbled on to outdoor development. Someone read an article about it. Then a mail shot from an outdoor development group, Impact Development Limited, came at the right moment to meet Haden's needs to have an outdoor development programme, which was intended:

1   to lay bare the management process in practice with something real;

2   to require task achievement with defined but limited resources;

3   to introduce *tolerable* stress and uncertainty; and

4   to set exercises in a framework that highlighted organisational and personal conflict, especially in team leaders.

Haden has only been using outdoor development since March 1983, but already they are committed to it and expanding their programme with senior managers (who also wanted the Board to take the course) to deal with risk management and the issue of delegation (why it is so difficult to do) as well as leadership.

John Sturla is still surprised at how effective the outdoor development has been. 'We found that many of our preconceived ideas about our colleagues were wrong.

There was no question of not talking to those of other culture groups. Nearly everyone during the week came up to their blocker and said "I can't do this, I can't go on", but there was no shame in that because during the week there were other tasks that depended on the same individuals and *they could* do it. We learned that everyone has his value, something to contribute. The question for the manager then is how can I harness it?[81]

7 The General Electric Company (GEC)

This is Britain's largest private employer with 178,000 employees. In 1983 GEC made a pre-tax profit of £670m on a turnover of £5.5 billion and spent over £700m in new plant, equipment and building, research and development. During the same period, GEC spent £49m on employee education and training.

160 companies make up the conglomerate as diverse as Schreiber furniture, Express Lifts and Marconi making a product range that runs from household furniture to guided missiles. Lord Weinstock and former Foreign Secretary Lord Carrington provide leadership at the top of GEC and a strong commitment to employee development which is shared by Board member, Mrs Sarah Morrison and Sir Richard Clayton.

GEC's commitment to outdoor development is embodied in Derek Webb, a full-time development training adviser. Based in the College of Management in Dunchurch outside Rugby, Mr Webb has been creating a series of development courses for GEC employees from apprentices and trainees to supervisors and managers over the last ten years. About 2,000 employees attend the courses each year provided by Dunchurch Lodge Services, the GEC training organisation. He uses the services of a half dozen outdoor development organisations:

> Adventure Sports Wales (ASW) Management
> Training Ltd
> Brathay Hall Trust
> Cornelyn Management Training

Development Training Ltd
Endeavour Training
Leadership Trust
Outward Bound.

The GEC's general management programme, leadership course, and the Dunchurch management development programme all contain 'supervised physical challenge tackling real problems in an outdoor setting'. This goes someway to answering a particular need in the company. As Derek Webb explained:

> Many of our people are thrust into management positions and have no idea of leadership or managerial responsibility and style. They are very highly skilled technologists and are quite accomplished from an academic point of view, but are simply not versed in leadership.
>
> I certainly believe very strongly that it's useful to take managers out of comfortable offices and to put them in a situation which is different and hostile, where decisions have to be made, communicative tools have to be used, and management nous has to be drawn on to achieve positive outcomes. You see how they react to new situations under a bit of pressure and it sticks in their memories with impact. There's a chance of cop-out in artificial classroom situations, which is not open to people in the outdoors where others are relying on your decisions and the penalties can be harsh.

In the GEC leadership course, four objectives are set out:

1   to help delegates to understand the responsibilities of a leader and to recognise and compare the effectiveness of different styles of leadership;
2   to develop each delegate's individual skills of leadership, including communication, delegation counselling, handling awkward situations;
3   to provide feedback on individual strengths and weaknesses and opportunities to work on these;
4   to get delegates to recognise the leaders' obligation to *do* things in order to get results.

Derek Webb sees relating the outdoor development programme to the work situation as the key to success in the training. It is extremely difficult, though, because 'many of the benefits of outdoor development training are not in many cases immediately tangible. I have seen within our GEC units an increasing acceptance of this type of training particularly amongst our younger managers. A number of managers in senior positions change their minds regarding the value of this type of development once they have actually seen and, in some cases, participated in an outdoor development course themselves.'

Ann Heine, a personnel officer, training at GEC's Easams Ltd, got direct experience of outdoor development at the Outward Bound Rhowniar Centre. There she shed the caricature image she had of Outward Bound and got some clearer ideas of how the outdoors is used for managerial development that is relevant to industry.

She expressed the resulting action of her immersion course in the following words: 'I have already spoken in some detail to my boss, the personnel manager, who while he apparently knew I would enjoy the experience, had not expected me to get so much from it. I believe he is now aware of: (a) how much I have benefited from my attendance; (b) the strength of my belief that Outward Bound has a place in the training of staff of our company. (I note now with interest that not only do Dunchurch management courses include this type of experience but, for example, so do Cranfield and Ashridge.)'

Her actions included active sponsorship of outdoor development courses within her firm. She was grateful for not only seeing another 'training tool' for their repertoire, but also for the rich personal benefits she gained.

Another believer in outdoor development, Jenny Duncan, a lecturer at the College of Management in Dunchurch, set up a women's outdoor development course in the spring of 1984 to give women a chance to experience the training as a group of women together, not in ones and twos, in a large group of employees. If the pilot is deemed effective it will be expanded.

A successful pilot project from 1983 linked GEC's outdoor development training to the company's sponsorship of camps for needy children at a residential centre owned by the Children's Aid Society at Winscombe in Somerset. GEC apprentices and trainees organised on their own and ran a camp for 50 deprived children in the summer of 1983. The camp staff of 20 was nominated from GEC companies across the country. They had two training weekends before the actual camp in which they were immediately given full responsibility for the project in all its details. Derek Webb and his advisers kept a low profile and simply let them get on with the election of a leader and the whole range of planning the securing of 'expert' staff members and the daily régime of the camp and later the actual execution of the plan. Three more camps run to that model are planned for the summer of 1984. The debriefing of the camp exercise takes place after the final day of the week-long camp in a hotel near the site where process issues and real experiential learning is summed up and fixed.

In the various forms of outdoor development he uses, Derek Webb has experienced solid success over the last ten years. He finds the outdoor experience for some a real conversion, a wrenching of a person from one direction to its opposite which he refers to as a 'road to Damascus experience'. For him, outdoor development is not a 'one shot in the arm event' but rather a 'structured ongoing development'. He uses no questionnaires to debrief or evaluate the experiences and is content with debriefings where participants simply sit around in peer groups to discuss the findings of the activities and processes they have undergone. One of the overarching goals of the development training is to tear down barriers erected over the decades. 'For a long time in this country we have manufactured our own barriers, slotting people into various categories', he said. 'You'll be a craft apprentice; you'll be a technician; you'll be a student and a graduate'. To break the mould, GEC mixed craft apprentices, technicians and graduates together on its development courses. He tells the story of how a gifted 23-year-old graduate, physically powerful and 'full of himself', took charge of a group on a week's outdoor development course. His group contained two craft apprentices, two technicians and a student and was doing very badly largely due to his authoritative approach – he made all decisions and ordered people about and they switched off and watched the achievement of the group nose-dive. Late in the week during an all-night exercise Derek Webb found the graduate lying in a ditch at 2.00 a.m. in a state of mental and physical exhaustion. A craft apprentice then took over the leadership of the group and it started to pick up instantly as he involved everyone and operated as a team with improved performance. To his credit, the recovering graduate saw the transformation in the group and took away from the experience an indelible lesson in avoiding the trap of autocratic leadership.

According to Derek Webb, the motivation of GEC for development training is to bind people to the company by showing care and concern for them as individuals. 'We're not just interested in them for their technical skills and knowledge. We want them to develop as persons. He does admit to some direct pay-offs for the company from such concern for employee development, notably faster growth in their management potential and more loyalty to company in resisting the lure to work for competitors.

He sees the future growth of outdoor development achieved only by vigorous education and promotional campaigns which would include:

1   decision makers in companies having the opportunity of participating in outdoor development schemes.
2   outdoor development workshops being organised for personnel and training managers;
3   the structured development training scheme which includes an outdoor element being implemented into young trainee, apprentice and graduate training programmes;
4   starting with the younger element of the workforce, where once the seeds are sown they will germinate and flourish. The message can then be spread.
5   keeping the outdoor element of development train-

ing as a small, integral part of the overall training programme.

He sums up by suggesting that the acceptance by companies regarding the value of outdoor development training will not be accomplished overnight. The objective must be a long-term one of spreading the gospel amongst the younger managers and employees.

8 Securicor

Securicor is the largest Security Company in the UK with overseas operations in Europe, the Middle East, Africa and Asia. In the Securicor Group there are companies as diverse as Phoenix World Travel (a travel agency), Pony Express International (motorcycle couriers) and London Hotels (an hotel group), but the main thrust of the group is in security services of all sorts from industrial property protection to cash carrying (about one billion pounds per week) from electronic surveillance systems to parcels delivery.

A more recent innovation is called Cellular Radio which will revolutionise the use of radio telephones. Securicor, who are themselves probably the largest two-way radio users of any private concern, have for many years offered the general public a range of mobile radio services. Now they are offering a selection of go-phones for the new Cellular Service – and they also have a joint company, with British Telecom, which will operate one of the two national cellular radio networks.

Overall, employees in the UK number about 20,000 including part-timers. The company's motto is 'Vigilant and Valiant' and its culture is broad based although with a strong leaning towards self discipline, due mainly to many managers at all levels having military or police backgrounds.

Securicor's path to outdoor development started in the Lake District at Brathay Hall Trust in 1978. At that time Andrew Brown, currently Securicor's National Training Manager, was director of training at Brathay Hall. Securicor's then General Manager and now Deputy Managing Director, Henry McKay, had heard about outdoor development from other sources. He sent a number of his managers to Brathay Hall and was so pleased with the management development Brathay provided that he took the opportunity of co-opting Andrew Brown, when his contract ended, to work for Securicor full-time. Today the company trains about 150 first line and middle managers using outdoor programmes. The benefits Securicor lists in order of importance are:

1 personal development;
2 communications workshop;
3 team development;
4 leadership development;
5 managing in uncertainty.

Their outdoor programmes are a combination of in-house courses, weekends at Brathay Hall directed by Henry McKay, and Brathay-run courses. Andrew Brown manages the outdoor development programme with staff he has helped to train to a level to meet Securicor's requirements.

In addition the company sends managers on a seven-day custom-tailored course at Brathay. These courses have special objectives. One designed for 21 participants is half from the operational side of Securicor and half from the financial side aimed at creating better worker relations between these two sides of the business.

As Andrew Brown explained: 'Securicor does not see these courses simply as outdoor courses. As important as the outdoor element are:

1 appropriate theoretical inputs by suitably qualified staff;
2 the elements of stretch – *mental and emotional* as well as physical – that are built into exercises and projects
3 the constructive and sensitive handling of review (post-experience) sessions run by tutors.

Outdoor exercises are certainly more closely related to

the nature of our business than is the case with other companies, but the main reason for using these establishments and techniques is that we believe the message is stronger and the effect longer-lasting'.

The commitment to outdoor development is a strong one and at least a day of outdoor learning is incorporated in every in-house management course usually using Richmond Park in Surrey.

'Our people must make decisions under duress and it can be a matter of life and death. Clear communications are critical and again must be made at times in dangerous and explosive situations', Andrew Brown explained.

9   Safeway Food Stores Ltd

Safeway is the world's largest food retailing group with over 2,300 supermarkets in the USA, Canada, Mexico, Australia, the Middle East, West Germany and the UK.

During its 22 years trading in Britain, Safeway introduced the American-style supermarket and has opened 108 stores in England and Scotland. With the slogan 'Everything you want from a store . . . and a little bit more,' Safeway continues to promote the concept of 'one-stop' shopping. The company employs 13,500 people including part-timers.

Alan Frost, training and development manager for Safeway, is responsible for the company's venture into outdoor development. His training as a police cadet, when he did the Duke of Edinburgh award up to gold standard, and five years' experience as a police officer in Surrey gave him some experience of outdoor development which lay dormant in his consciousness for years.

As he explained it, Safeway had always been involved in leadership programmes like action centred leadership (ACL) and training within industry (TWI), run by the Manpower Services Commission.

> Two-and-a-half years ago I was dissatisfied with what we were doing to develop our managers. The courses were well received. Everyone was satisfied. But I was

troubled and concerned with the relationship between what we were telling these people and the sort of job they actually did. Most of them are store managers – people who are used to being on their feet and on the move very much in a dynamic management role rather than a desk-bound role.

We were talking to them about concepts such as morale and we had great difficulty in putting it over as an abstract concept. Everyone would sit and nod their heads wisely as if to say 'yes, we know all about morale'. But I had this gut feeling that they didn't really appreciate what high or low morale could do to an organisation or the interaction between morale and performance. The closest we got to it was building a tower of Lego bricks. If the tower of bricks fell over everybody had a good laugh and the builder got a bit of ribbing from the other teams, but he suffered no more, and he didn't get an appreciation of 'morale'.

The same was true of leadership, and the person could be the worst leader on earth and he didn't see the effects of bad leadership in the warm classroom with Lego towers crashing around him.

Alan Frost had just returned from such a session when he called in one of his training officers to discuss it. They decided to try an outdoor development programme in Ashdown Forest in Sussex. They designed a one-day event to replace the Lego tower exercise and have never looked back.

The courses run all year round in all weathers: 'In wintertime they work in darkness for about two hours,' Alan Frost explained. 'The outdoors programmes really brought out concepts such as morale and group cohesion, especially if it was cold and wet and they could see the morale of the group dropping like a stone in water when they got lost and were cold with rain dripping down their necks. They could see groups start to fall apart.'

'As a leader the person had to get his group out of a difficult position. He couldn't just say "Well, there go a lot of Lego bricks all over the floor! "'

From the beginning, these outdoor development programmes were run with only two staff members from the training department. Participants were divided into three teams with one student observer assigned to each team. Since the exercise had each team covering ten miles in three different directions, the staff depended on the student observer for feedback comments as well as on the assigned team leaders.

At first, the participants were management trainees with an age spread of 18–mid–30s with the bulk of trainees in the 18–24 age band. But word of the effectiveness of the programme spread throughout the company and soon there was a demand for outdoor development for the store managers and later for the department heads within Safeway's 108 stores. Among the management trainees, 15–20 per cent of the participants are women. The ratio falls to 10 per cent among the department managers and takes a further dip with store managers.

As the outdoor development programme grew, the company searched for and found the Bernard Sunley Activity Centre, an outdoor facility in Ashdown Forest run under the auspices of the London Federation of Boys' Clubs. The training and development manager felt the 10-mile orienteering he had set for his participants taxed their physical stamina but not their minds. With the help of the professional outdoor staff, he cut down on the distances they had to travel while increasing the mental rigour of the exercises. The legend used in the early days of Safeway's outdoor programmes had the participants working covertly in the countryside as SAS teams which did not communicate with the locals and regarded everyone else as the 'enemy'. The role playing becomes very 'real' and the sound of someone coming down a country lane prompted one member of the team to leap straight over a high hedge to avoid detection by an 'enemy agent' who later turned out to be a lady with a pram. The mission was to collect three sections of a nose cone to a rocket which looks remarkably like a common red and white traffic cone, a wooden box and a 45-gallon oil drum.

Inputs from full-time professional outdoor development staff lately have brought more sophistication to the tasks. Rather crude outdoor challenges like getting an oil drum across a stream were refined to adventure-based exercises. Now, codes lodged in inaccessible places have to be broken to work out clues as to where the treasure lies. Teams have to negotiate progress on projects and the 'Krypton factor' has been raised.

Safeway is clear about what it wants from outdoor development. In the early days Alan Frost asked a representative of a commercial adventure training facility what the benefit of the courses was, and was told that the participants 'go away knowing a lot more about themselves'. He does not deride self-knowledge and personal growth. "We want the accent to be on team building and leadership not on personal growth. As a company we didn't want to spend £1000 per head for simply an increase in self-awareness'.

Safeway is looking for a powerful experience of teamwork from outdoor development which will help its managers maintain high morale in its stores. For instance when a new store opens sparkling teamwork shines from the staff. The store manager radiates confidence as he sees his sales break records. Maintaining high morale is easy in those artificial circumstances. The challenge for store management arises when within weeks sales slide down to more realistic levels and the glitter of a grand opening is over. It is then that a store manager digs deep into his reserves to find hidden springs of energy perhaps first discovered leading a dispirited team through the thick undergrowth of Ashdown Forest.

10   Union International

Union International is one of the UK's largest privately controlled group of companies with 36,000 employees worldwide and an annual turnover of £856.4 million. Within the Union International Group are many operating companies whose activities span beef production to pharmaceuticals, knitting wool to refrigerated transport.

Its central business is the production and processing of animal products for food. From the ranch to the butcher's shop this sprawling multinational is a classic example of backward and foreward integration. The Dewhurst chain of high street shops is where the public directly meets Union International.

Union International is one of the first companies in the UK to use outdoor development for its managers and over the decade has designed unique features in its training programmes.

At the outset the group training department used the programmes provided by organisations like Brathay Hall Trust. They did not tamper with the courses for their young employees provided by these organisations which are experts in youth training. But they soon were redesigning activities to achieve specific objectives on courses for their seasoned managers. Today the company designs its own ten-day managers' courses at sites run by Outward Bound, Brathay Hall Trust, Cornelyn Manor and other organisations. Peter Hanley, recruiting and development manager, described the ten-day course which aims to make sure that the exercises 'are closer to and more recognisable to business situations'. On the site of the outdoor development organisation, company trainers provide a two-and-a-half day introduction to the course which includes 'build-up exercises' run by outdoor experts. 'The main object of the entire ten-day exercise', Peter Hanley explained, 'is for the course members to set up a "company" to carry out work which has been set in conjunction with the organisations'. The outdoor development organisation, in fact, becomes the 'customer' that the 'company' must satisfy. A win-win situation develops in which the organisation has something useful that they wanted done accomplished, while the course participants feel the constraints and challenge of achieving a real objective. Union International employees on such courses have built concrete slipways into lakes, constructed permanent bridges, rebuilt a boathouse, restored crumbling buildings for living quarters, designed stores and planned materials handling, developed entire marketing plans for organisations and built an army-style assault course. A full day is spent debriefing the project. This day Peter Hanley believes is the most important of the ten-day course. The debriefing takes place on site or nearby and is an intensive learning experience.

Something of the boldness of this approach to outdoor development and the power of the practical projects can be seen from the following project brief on the Union International managing people leadership course run at Cornelyn Manor 22nd–31st March 1983.

Project brief: adventure course development company (ACDC)

Your group is to operate as a company which you are required to set up in order to carry out the task as detailed below.

Background to your task.

'The Cornelyn Manor Business Centre' is a relatively young private venture using property and accommodation of a much older vintage. Obviously, following the initial expenditure, it is necessary to keep costs to a minimum and so it is essential that the most efficient use be made of the present facilities.

As well as running its own leadership courses, Cornelyn Manor is also an outdoor activity centre for a cross-section of all ages and varying physical capabilities. There are already in existence exercises and activities which occupy a whole day and others which can be completed very quickly. What is needed is something which can occupy a good proportion of half a day, alternatively be adapted for shorter leadership-style exercises, or equally just be for fun and personal achievement.

Your task

To design then construct as much as possible, if not all, of an army style assault training course within the grounds of

Cornelyn Manor in the area indicated on the enclosed map known as the Owls Copse.

The course must be as safe as is reasonably practicable and should include a rope swing or traverse over a water-filled pit, a Burma rope bridge, a 12-foot high wood or brick 'smooth' climbing wall as an exercise for scaling without equipment, plus an aerial runway.

Once set up, the equipment must be such that no part of the participant's body is allowed to touch the ground once the first exercise has commenced until the whole course has been completed.

Project presentations

Your clients, who include the UI staff, require and expect a presentation of your findings and proposals, which should include a budget for approval, at a mutually agreed time on Sunday morning, if not earlier. This should certainly take place no later than 11.30 a.m. at least not without adequate reason and explanation. For this presentation you will be expected to use visual aids as appropriate in explaining your ideas, e.g. plans, drawings, scale models, artists' impressions, etc.

The final presentation of your work will take place on Wednesday morning at 9 o'clock. At this presentation you are required to have available a full written report to which your clients can refer after your departure. This is most important. As well as showing all costs incurred and work carried out, this report should include any further proposals and future recommendations.

Organisation

How you arrange the resources within the group is for you to decide, but:

1   You will initially operate with a management team of two. This does not prohibit other members of the group being coopted into this management team should it be thought necessary.
2   A detailed organisation plan must be in the hands of

the UI training staff before breakfast on Saturday. After this you will not be allowed to proceed any further with your project until this information is forthcoming.

3 Your customer throughout the whole of this task is one of the directors of Cornelyn Manor Business Centre, Mr B. E. Thorogood. Like any other customer in industry or commerce, Barry Thorogood, owner and director of Cornelyn Manor, is a busy man with other commitments. This means that his time available to you is limited and he does not want all and sundry approaching him for whatever reason at all times of the day. You are required, therefore, to elect one person who will act as your liaison man with your customer. He has asked that more general meetings with the whole or part of the group should be by prior appointment only, preferably with at least 12 hours' notice.

4 Neither Barry Thorogood, his staff, the UI training staff, nor the observers are to be considered as part of the workforce.

Constraints:

1 Once your proposals have been accepted, tree branches may be trimmed, if necessary, but only with your client's approval and on no account should any trees be felled.

2 For details of financial constraints please see 'General information' and remember that you should be working at all times to an agreed budget.

3 Should it be necessary for any of you to leave the centre at any time, it is essential that you keep the UI training staff informed of your movements.

4 You should bear in mind at all times that, along with all others at work in Britain, you must comply with the Health and Safety at Work Act 1974 with regard both to the safety of yourselves and others.

5 Accordingly, once your plans have been approved, the work site itself will be designated a hard hat area.

Anyone failing to wear a protective helmet whilst work is being carried out above them will be asked to remove themselves from the vicinity until they are suitably attired.

General information:

1 You may find that some material, tools and equipment are available on request from your client or the UI staff; the majority may have to be purchased. Whatever you do as regards supplies, you should first check with Barry Thorogood or the UI training staff.

2 All purchases, where possible, must be made through and/or approved by the customer. If this is not possible, authorisation must be obtained from the UI training staff who hold a petty cash float available to you. The use of this petty cash float is at the discretion of your 'company manager' and 'accountant' but, as a guide, should be looked upon as a last resort if your client or the UI staff are unavailable. *No major purchases* should be made this way. Full details must be provided of *all* items of expenditure as part of your presentation to the UI staff at the end of the project. It is essential that receipts be obtained for all cash purchases otherwise reimbursement might not be possible.

3 During the course of the project you may well wish to contact or visit other organisations. Before doing so will you please discuss this with Barry Thorogood, or the UI staff, who may be able to help you.

4 With regard to the aerial runway, you are to aim for the longest achievable length but, for safety reasons, it is desirable that its route does not take it over any other exercises or pieces of equipment of the assault course.

5 Your hours of work are totally flexible (with the exception of meals) and are under your control. Should you be unable to construct all of the course during the total time available to you, your client

reserves the right upon consultation to decide which pieces of apparatus should receive priority. He would, of course, like the course to be completed in its entirety.

The project is deliberately too vast for the group of 12–16 people to finish by working 9 to 5. Hence it requires high commitment and motivation, leadership, teamwork, skills in decision making, communication and time management and meticulous planning.

About half of the workforce in the UK is in Dewhurst, 6,500–7,000 people. Adrian Owen, who in the 1960s was an Outward Bound instructor for four years with experience in four different schools, and is now training manager for Dewhurst, is constructively critical of the role of outdoor development instructors:

> They're smashing people and they say they can relate the outdoor experience to work, but they have limited direct experience of the business world and industrial environment. They don't understand the subtle difference between manufacturing unit, a small or large one, the totally different problems of running units that are geographically scattered, the feel, the temperament of people in research and development as opposed to that of people in high street trading.

Another difficulty Adrian Owen identified is the tendency of outdoor development organisations to get into a rut and serve up the same programme, which they do well, to meet any management need.

The need Union International has for projects means that they have an insatiable appetite for outdoor development organisations that have meaningful projects they want completed and who are willing to pay for materials.

Seasoned managers who have been managing people for 20 years and suddenly find themselves on the 'other side of the fence' in a project effort are often amazed at what it is like. Often they say things in the debriefing which acknowledges progress in their attitudes, e.g. 'I realise how when I treat people badly the negative effect it has on them'. This is said by many managers after the experience.

When the projects are as real as building a slipway into a lake, the lessons to be learned about management style and authority and human motivation can be powerful. 'Theory X' and 'theory Y' approaches to managing people are put to the test. A manager's potential for participative decision-making is on trial.

Lessons are learned by the 'workers' as well. On one occasion the unionised building crew refused to wear weatherproofs, but instead negotiated a wet and dirty rate for the job. By the time the negotiations were completed, with the management conceding a substantial payment, the 'workers' were so wet they were not in a fit state to continue the work.

Other lessons come from experiencing management styles. 'What were the problems working with this management team?' is one of the questions put to the 'workers' in the debriefing. The 'managers' are asked what they would do differently in managing the project if they were to do it again. But significantly they are also asked what they would do the same. Peter Hanley explained: 'If you ask only questions that lead them to think negatively, they ignore the positive side of what they did well which is important'.

Adrian Owen added, 'They learn industrial relations through experience. At work they might think "the lads wouldn't wear that", but on the project they think "well, I've got to try to get them to wear it and of course, they find they can"'.

The debriefing day is 'out of bounds' for visitors who may be allowed to watch them work on the project. The time is too important and the role of the trainers becomes that of facilitators to get them to debrief themselves. 'They will be critical of themselves and their conduct over the last five days', Adrian Owen said, 'but we have to be careful we don't let them plough themselves into the ground. They must see what they did well'.

Outdoor development at Union International has become so much a part of the company culture – the normal way they do things – that an ASTMS representative in one of the cold storage companies requested that a supervisor go on the course to become part of the in-crowd who have experienced the development programme. 'When he comes into the mess and we're discussing a problem and drawing parallels with a [outdoor development] project, he doesn't have a clue what we're talking about', the union representative said. All the signs point to a continuation of outdoor development at Union International and a further evolution of a progressive, positive and innovative form of management development in the out-of-doors.

OUTDOOR DEVELOPMENT ORGANISATIONS

Brathay Hall Trust, Leadership Trust and Outward Bound were the 'big three' organisations which were mentioned most frequently in my research by the companies who use outdoor development. But a surprising number of companies (13) used their own in-house resources for outdoor development and many other organisations as well. Hence two dozen other outdoor development organisations were mentioned.

Most of these organisations are described in this chapter, yet the list in no way attempts to cover all consultants who do this type of training and all outdoor development organisations in the UK. It is at best a partial map.

APN Development Training

34A Greenway Gardens
Greenford

Middlesex UB6 9TT
01 578 0093

APN works with a sponsor to design courses to meet the needs they identify. It runs company management programmes as well as youth development training for supervisors and trainees. Its repertoire includes action learning, life and social skills, adventure experience, and interactive skills, as well as management development.

Alternative Development Training

41 London Road
Maldon
Essex CM29 6HS
(0621) 52603/54725

In its courses for middle managers and executives, Alternative Development Training focuses on project work management. A single project is planned and carried out by the delegates during the six-day courses. The financial aspects of the projects are integrated with outdoor activities. Another six-day course is aimed at developing managerial skills. It features a number of interrelated projects, some indoors and some out-of-doors, to stimulate personal development and group dynamics.

For the youth end of the market, YTS delegates, apprentices, etc., Alternative Development Training runs a four-day programme during summer months only which involves a camping journey with progressively more difficult tasks to be performed. Stress situation and recreation are blended to foster both personal and group development.

Alternative also runs tailor-made courses for companies and in-company work.

Brathay Hall Trust

Brathay Hall

Ambleside
Cumbria LA22 0HP
09663 3041

The Brathay Hall Trust, like Outward Bound, is an organisation established in 1946 for the education and personal development of young people. Brathay Hall bases its
activities on a 300-acre estate of parkland and woods on
the shores of Windermere in the Lake District National
Park.

For management development Brathay offers a range of
courses:

> Leadership in action (6 days)
> Managers in action (6 days)
> Supervisors in action (6 days)

For young people there are three courses:

> Preparing for leadership (12 days)
> Responsibility at work (14 days)
> Team building (4 days)

Each course is targeted to a specific group and has its own
objectives. The managers in action course, for example, is
for experienced and practising managers with direct
responsibility for staff employees, supervisors or other
managers; technologists or specialists who are about to
broaden their management responsibilities.

The objectives of the course are:

1   to develop skills in getting results through people:
    as the leader of a group; as a decision maker; as a
    communicator; or as an effective group member;
2   to demonstrate to managers that change is an
    opportunity instead of a threat;
3   to provide an opportunity for self-assessment.

The course was designed over five years with the consultation of Professor John Adair and uses his action-centred
leadership model. The participants return with action
plans.

The supervisors in action course is aimed at men and

women (with preferably at least two years' experience) with *current* responsibilities for direct supervision in factories, offices and shops.

The objectives are:

1 to develop an understanding of the skills of good leadership;
2 to develop the skills needed to cope positively with change at the supervisor's level;
3 to develop the capacity to communicate, including sensitivity to the supervisor's training function;
4 to develop self-confidence;
5 to provide an opportunity for self-assessment.

To take just one of the youth-orientated courses, responsibility at work is geared to 16–21-year-olds under job/skill training or in junior positions at work, craft apprentices, technicians, retail trainees, bank trainees, clerks/typists, commercial trainees, operatives and process workers, and clerical workers. The course objectives are:

1 to develop personal potential;
2 to provide a clear understanding of the responsibilities of all the individuals within an effective working group;
3 to develop the ability and willingness to communicate;
4 to build self-confidence;
5 to encourage high personal standards.

Clients for Brathay Hall courses include British Telecom, British Home Stores, Union International, Hargreaves Group, Pilkington Group, Silentnight Holdings Ltd, Plessey Telecommunications.

Bristol Polytechnic

South West Management Centre
Coldharbour Lane
Frenchay
Bristol BS16 1QY
Bristol (0272) 656 261 Ext. 286.

Development training courses, incorporating use of the outdoors, are designed on learning objectives which are jointly formulated with the client.

Course aims are twofold, based at an individual and a group level. At the *individual* level they seek to:

1 increase confidence and maximise self-potential;
2 increase self-awareness and personal insight into strengths and weaknesses;
3 develop individual leadership skills.

At the *group* level they seek to:

1 increase trust and cooperation;
2 increase the group's ability to manage its own process of communication, decision making and problem solving;
3 build a team.

The main elements of the courses are as follows:

1 practical exercises both indoors and outdoors designed to generate a wide range of relevant experience within the group setting;
2 review sessions embracing group discussions and formal feedback from tutors designed to maximise learning and the relationship between experience and theory;
3 an introduction to the theoretical basis of group behaviour and leadership patterns as a response to issues arising from identified needs;
4 personal development sessions during which individuals receive feedback from their colleagues on their performance and combine this with self-appraisal to produce an action plan of personal development needs;
5 follow-up sessions conducted, if there is demand, in-company to aid transference of learning to the work situation and to further assist with individual development needs.

The participants are housed in Felixstowe Court in the

management residential unit of the Polytechnic and make trips to the Forest of Dean and the Wye Valley.

Clients include ICI and the Department of Management Studies.

Celmi Adventure Education

Llanegryn
Tywyn
Gwynedd LL36 9SA
Tywyn (0654) 710609

Celmi operates outdoor development courses from a very old, traditional Welsh farmhouse and outbuildings on the west coast of Wales in the Snowdonia National Park. The farm looks out over the Dysynsi Valley towards Craig-y-Deryn and 3,000 ft high Cader Idris. Its outdoor activities include: rock climbing, abseiling, mountain walking, canoeing (on estuary, river, sea or white water) orienteering, camping, swimming, sailing, ropes and assault courses, slate and gold mine exploration, river descents, rafting, pony trekking, and survival exercises. It has an impressive array of cultural, creative, academic and social activities.

The spectacular beauty of the area is rivalled by the great variety of the physical landscape. The sparse population consists of farmers, shepherds and quarrymen who cooperate with Celmi and give them easy access to the land.

The courses for managers last between 48 and 72 hours. Celmi claims to use 'the outdoors and culture shock in an imaginative and supportive way to develop some of the most senior managers in British industry and commerce'. Its closed company programmes are designed to assist 'in the process of unfreezing during organisational change, to gain access to greater creativity, to develop individual risk taking and to motivate teams towards understanding synergy'.

The Celmi experience also claims 'to develop team synergy, to expose latent talent, to heal personality clashes, to foster harmony between departments, to enhance personal understanding and to improve communication and trust'.

A selected sample of Celmi's clients used the organisation for the following varied objectives:

1   to accelerate the merger of two advertising agencies and to decrease the anxiety that exists;
2   to reduce inter-departmental barriers and to encourage more open collaboration;
3   to bring together a group of managers geographically dispersed, prior to a major product launch;
4   to strengthen relationships between their company and its clients;
5   to unfreeze old ways prior to a change in the company and individual management styles;
6   to allow the cast of a West End play to come together;
7   to allow employees to get to know, understand and appreciate each other outside of their office roles.

Although its literature smacks of oversell, Celmi's list of clients is impressive. It includes:

Allied Breweries
American Express
BBC
Berger Paints
Computer and Systems Engineering
Chetwynd Haddons
International Exporters
Mars Confectionery
Mars Group Services
Northern Telecom
Tetley Walker

Challenge Training Limited

Isabella Mews

The Avenue
Combe Down
Bath BA2 5EM
Bath (0225) 835 448

Challenge Training specialises in using the outdoors to provide development programmes to help working teams and individual managers to practise and improve their skills in:

1   solving problems and making decisions;
2   planning and coordinating;
3   working with and through others;
4   influencing and leading;
5   managing uncertainty and change;
6   taking calculated risks.

The organisation generally does not run open program-mes where a company can send one or two delegates. Rather the programmes are tailor-made for clients to ensure relevance and transferability back to the company. They like to work closely with a firm's internal trainers.

Challenge programmes are 'based on learning by doing rather than on learning by listening; this is because the practical value of learning the skills of managing lies in what people do differently afterwards rather than in what they know'.

The group becomes the main vehicle for learning in the Challenge approach to development. Debriefing as usual in outdoor development is done in the group. The reviews centre on:

1   the processes of agreeing the objectives and the strategy within the group;
2   the relationship between sub-groups;
3   the relationship between the centre and these sub-groups;
4   group and team skills appropriate to the situation.

Challenge Training chooses not to have its own site, but rather to operate from a fleet of vehicles that carry its equipment to a convenient place for the client. Its major clients include: American Express, British Aerospace, British Petroleum, Elanco Products Ltd, and Unigate.

Cornelyn Manor

Llangoed
Beaumaris
Anglesey
Gwynedd LL58 8SB
Llangoed (024878) 444

Cornelyn Manor promotes an open course 'adventure-based management' which runs a full five days. They claim to use 'modern methods of learning harnessed to traditional business ethics' to produce in managers the qualities of 'leadership, trust and dependability'. They work to an action-centred leadership model and make extensive use of debriefing. Based in a manor house that has access to both sea and mountains, Cornelyn Manor designs courses around outdoor tasks which include canoeing, sailing, caving and climbing. Clients for the open course include TSB and Marconi.

They also run closed courses for a minimum of 16 delegates. Their closed course clients include Taylor Woodrow, Plessey, Smiths Industries and Abbott Laboratories, the Union International Company Ltd (which includes Dewhurst).

Dalguise Centre

Dunkeld
Perthshire
Scotland
(03502) 339

The Dalguise Centre is based in an old family manor house on an 80-acre site of land. The mansion can accommodate up to 80 people.

Dalguise Centre provides residential experience for the youth end of the training market. But it also has the capability to design outdoor development courses for management.

Its principal outdoor activities include orienteering and rock climbing. Craig-y-barnes is a local crag and the Ben Lawes mountain is nearby. There is also sailing and canoeing on Loch Tag and the River Tag and the River Lyon. Its main company clients include: British Steel; ICI and National Steel.

Development Training Ltd

68 Oakfield Road
Clifton
Bristol
0272 641422

Development Training Ltd has its own site for outdoor development courses at Ardwyn House, Llanwrtyd Wells in mid-Wales. It designs courses to meet company needs and will conduct them in company training centres. The programmes vary from long weekend courses, Thursday evening through to Sunday, to the five-day working week courses. Seven to ten-day courses are also on offer.

Development Training works with all levels of managers. Its main clients include Rolls Royce, GEC, British Aerospace, the Post Office, and Nestles Co. at Rolls Royce Development Training has responsibility for all apprentice development which includes 1,200 – 1,500 apprentices each year making it the largest apprentice programme in Europe.

Endeavour Training

17a Glumangate
Chesterfield
Derbyshire S40 1TX

Endeavour Training is a national voluntary organisation. Founded in 1955, its work and concerns are directed into six main channels:

1   MSC programmes;
2   management development;
3   community and inner city needs;
4   education;
5   expeditions;
6   people at work.

It is funded in part by the Department of Education and Science, the Manpower Services Commission and by donations and earnings from industry, trusts, and members of the public. Endeavour's work in personal development is strongly supported by some of the largest companies in industry where it is incorporated into the training of their own employees: apprentices, shop assistants, supervisors and managers.

Training is based on the use of residential courses, the costs of which are met by the user company. Endeavour provides opportunities for continuing personal development, on a voluntary basis, through the National Endeavour Training Association (NETA).

Courses can be tailored to an individual company's special requirements. A typical outdoor development course for a company would have aims that go beyond personal development. Concentrating in the main on active learning situations and processes, delegates on a course, for example, designed to foster leadership would be given many opportunities to examine, question and test the following:

1   leadership qualities;
2   the application of those qualities to achieve successful results.
3   styles of leadership to suit particular situations.
4   the importance of a personal and honest appraisal of the experiences;
5   the resilience of the individual in the leadership process.

As a result of attending the course, delegates should be able to:

1 demonstrate their understanding of leadership qualities, principles and techniques, and their relevance to the work place;
2 show that they have achieved a greater understanding and awareness of themselves particularly in relation to 'personal strengths and attributes';
3 demonstrate a greater awareness of effective communication skills;
4 show that they understand how to structure and programme introductory leadership training opportunities for first-, second- and third-year trainees;
5 appreciate the value of personal development techniques, using experiential methods, generally in the outdoors, and in relation to confidence, esteem and achievement;
6 demonstrate their understanding of the 'curriculum approach to development training' in the form of preparation, experience, reflection, learning;
7 appreciate the nature of group work and sensitivity.

Among the many clients of Endeavour are:

Henry Boot & Sons
British Aerospace
British Telecom
J. H. Dewhurst
Galliford & Sons
Midland Bank
Metal Box
Norwich Union Insurance Group
Post Office
Proctor & Gamble

Fallbarrow Training

Dove Nest Management Centre
Dove Nest

Windermere
Cumbria LA23 1LR

Fallbarrow Training offers courses for managers, junior managers, supervisors and apprentices using a new management training centre recently established by Cumbria Outdoor Pursuits Ltd to cater for the increasing demand for developmental courses using the outdoors. The centre is an 18th century house that stands in 60 acres of land on the southern slopes of Wansfell, midway between Windermere and Ambleside.

Fallbarrow Training provides both open and closed or in-company courses. The management course is designed for men and women involved in all levels of management where they have the responsibility for the effective use of resources and people. It creates a stressful environment in which participants must work together to achieve objectives. Real problems are presented for solution where communications, flexibility and positive commitment are required for decision making. The participants are guided in ongoing assessment of themselves and their teams and the situations are related to the work environment.

The objectives are:

1   to develop management skills;
2   to develop an awareness of change and its consequences;
3   to develop an appreciation of strengths and weaknesses of others;
4   to develop an appreciation of strengths and weaknesses in themselves.

The supervisors' courses for those engaged in supervisory roles, whether new to the job or seasonal, has the following objectives:

1   to recognise and to develop leadership potential;
2   to develop powers of application;
3   to gain an appreciation of the importance and effect of interpersonal relations;
4   to increase understanding of the changes which can

occur when operating under stress;

5 to realise the necessity for cooperation and team-work;

6 to develop communication skills.

Clients include Silentnight Holdings and Layezee

Impact Development Training Group

Blackwell
Windermere
Cumbria LA23 3JR

Impact individually tailors courses to meet the specific objectives of their clients. They offer four distinct types of programmes:

1 management development – aimed at senior and middle management decision makers and planners;

2 supervisory development – geared for managers at supervisory level and focusing on leadership, communication and planning skills; also some conflict management;

3 team development – for both newly formed teams such as resulting from mergers or new companies and relatively well-established working groups;

4 young people's development, designed to help youth make the transition from home and school to the workplace.

In their approach they do not attempt to teach techniques but rather to develop skills through experience and reflection. As a matter of policy, Impact does not operate from its own property. Instead it uses the Lake District National Park and local hotels, claiming to have invested its money not on a residential property but rather in the latest equipment for outdoor development. GEC is one of Impact's clients.

The Industrial Society

Peter Runge House

3 Carlton House Terrace
London SW1Y 5DG
01 839 4300

The Industrial Society as an option runs a few of its action-centred leadership (ACL) courses out-of-doors. These outdoor development ACL modules are run by the management and training adviser. They consist of one-and-a-half days indoors in which the standard course is taught; followed by two days of outdoor activities which take place on an outdoor site lent to the Industrial Society by a local authority East Sussex fire brigade. Richard Boult, management and training adviser, summed up the activities: 'they are about building a structure, moving a structure or finding something' that create 'the shared experience which we can then talk about'. Motivation problems around the ALC concept and communication problems are felt to be more dramatic in the out-of-doors. Debriefing is central to the course and confidentiality between the Industrial Society staff and the students is a priority. No report back on the delegates or assessment is made to the sponsor companies.

The Industrial Society does not intend to rival outdoor development organisations. Its emphasis on the courses is not personal development but rather simply raising the pitch of its action-centred leadership course. On request the outdoor design of the ACL course can be tailored to meet a client's needs.

The Leadership Trust

Symonds Yat West
Ross-on-Wye
Herefordshire HR9 6BL
0600 890696

The Leadership Trust is a pioneer in using outdoor development training for industry, commerce and the public services. Founded nine years ago in 1975 by David

Gilbert-Smith, chief executive, the Trust deals with over a thousand delegates a year and serves over 150 different companies and organisations including business schools and universities.

The Trust's objectives are to promote leadership and provide comprehensive training in order to:

1 define and develop personal leadership abilities and build self-confidence in leading people;
2 broaden the knowledge and understanding of the nature and functions of leadership;
3 develop the ability to build and harness cohesive teams to achieve common objectives;
4 create an open style of leadership based on integrity; effective two-way communication; initiative; accepting responsibility; making decisions and taking action.

The Trust's approach to leadership development starts with the premise that people have leadership ability within them to a greater or lesser degree; that in some circumstances – family, work, sports or social – a person is sometimes leader, sometimes follower. We develop our effectiveness at leadership and followership (upwards leadership) by awareness of our 'personal power' (influence), realisation of our natural strengths, control of our vulnerabilities, and by practising and improving our handling of people in the various situations and pressures that confront us. Leadership is not a subject that can be formally taught. It is a continuous process of acquiring and developing knowledge, skills and attitudes; with guidance and direction by skilled tutors.

The stages of leadership development covered by Trust courses are:

1 developing personal leadership ability and subsequent personal development programmes;
2 team building and team leadership;
3 organisational leadership;

The Trust's strategy is to enable people to practise and learn leadership for themselves in real and closely monitored situations where it is safe to fail. These situations are specifically designed and programmed to recreate pressures and problems similar to work, but in a different environment using different vehicles. This approach highlights the learning values and gives immediate and long-lasting impact.

After every practical experience there is a comprehensive review, carefully directed by skilled and qualified tutors, to draw out the learning points and define improvements both for personal and team development.

The leadership in management course is specifically designed to give the initial intensive training necessary to start the whole process of leadership development. The Trust then provides post-course follow-up, team building, and special courses as required, to help each stage of personal and team growth.

The courses offered include:

Leadership in management (5½ days)
This draws on a wide variety of learning vehicles both indoor and outdoor, to include activities such as diving, climbing and canoeing. The course is designed to provide learning for mixed management levels.

Leadership in management (3½ days)
This is designed for managers who seek to practise and further develop their leadership and team-building abilities without recourse to physical activities.

Leadership and transactional analysis (1 day)
This one-day course teaches the use of transactional analysis as a vehicle to develop self-awareness, self-control and leadership ability in handling people. Its programme complements the leadership in management courses.

Special and mobile courses and in-company courses
Special courses are designed to meet the particular needs of individual organisations. These may be run at the Leadership Trust Centre at Symonds Yat or by using the

Trust's mobile equipment at member organisations' own training centre or adjacent hotel. The latter is particularly valuable for linking in modular training in-company and for practical sessions on annual conferences. The Trust specialises in running short courses for boards of directors or for top teams.

Personal leadership development course (2½ days)
This course is designed for the next progressive stage of development for post-leadership in management (5½- and 3½-day) course delegates. There is further input for personal development and team building which includes new projects providing more learning opportunities in new situations. There are additional aspects of mirror and reviewing to enable greater personal feedback and further develop team-handling abilities.

Leadership Trust does not have its own residential facilities but makes use of a hotel at the edge of its headquarters.

A list of its company clients reads like a catalogue of household names in British industry and commerce.

Lindley Lodge Educational Trust Ltd

Head Office:
Watling Street
Nuneaton
Warwickshire CV10 0TZ
Nuneaton (0682) 348 128

Lindley Lodge, founded in 1970, operates from three residential training centres in Nuneaton, Hollowford, in the centre of the Derbyshire Peak District which specialises in outdoor activities, and Swinton. Three thousand five hundred young people attend courses at the centre each year sponsored by over 200 companies across British industry and commerce. Many of the courses have a substantial element of outdoor development.

Lindley Lodge is an independent, charitable, Christian

trust whose governing council consists of people from industry, commerce, trade unions, education and the church.

Young employees, according to Lindley Lodge, receive the following benefits from its courses:

1   a better understanding of themselves;
2   greater skills in relating to and working with others;
3   more ability to exercise authority and respond to it;
4   greater ability to adjust to their work environment.

Lindley runs both open courses and three 12-day separate courses according to a company's needs. The open courses include:

1   a general course for all young employees aged 16–19 (6 days);
2   a general course for all young employees aged 17–22 (12 days);
3   a course for technician apprentices aged 19–22 (6 days);
4   a course for graduates during their first year at work (6 days);
5   a course for training instructors and supervisors (3 days).

Lindley Lodge's many clients include:

British Steel Corporation
Delta Metal
GEC
ICI
Marks & Spencer
NCB
Industrial training Boards.

Outdoor Development Limited

Bay View
Cliff Road
Laugharne
Dyfed

South Wales
(099421) 393
London office 01 341 4349. Oxfordshire Office: MRA
International, (0235) 81–2026

Outdoor Development Limited's activities are run from a
19th century Welsh house on a cliff overlooking the
estuary of the River Taf leading to Carmarthen Bay in
Laugharne, South Wales. The town is at the eastern end of
the seven-mile stretch of sands which end at Pendine. A
few miles beyond are the coastal resorts of Saundersfoot
and Tenby with sailing harbours leading to the Irish Sea.

Outdoor Development Limited makes use of the easy
access to the sea for sailing activities and scuba-diving and
numerous rivers for canoeing. The nearby Pembrokeshire
Coast National Park is used for orienteering. Pen-y-fan at
over 2,900 feet and Black Mountain at 2,600 feet provide
dramatic mountain experiences in the Brecon Beacons.

The organisation does not run open courses, but rather
custom tailors outdoor development programmes to
meet clients' needs. The staff is mobile and will design
programmes in other parts of the country more convenient to the client. Part of Outdoor Development Limited's philosophy maintains that the outdoors environment for the courses should be unfamiliar to the participants and rather spectacular in natural beauty. This they
maintain 'wrenches the participants from their normal
familiar surroundings and forces them to cope with
situations in an environment which can be as fierce as it is
beautiful'.

Outward Bound Trust

12 Upper Belgrave Street
London SW1X 8BA
01 235 4286

Outward Bound Trust is a registered charity that has

pioneered outdoor development courses since 1941. On the open courses for youth sponsorship is 80 per cent industry and commerce from companies as diverse as Barclays Bank and the National Coal Board. Outward Bound deals with all levels of employee in its courses from youth courses with apprentices, clerks, supervisors, graduate trainees, YTS delegates and the unemployed, to management courses designed for a company's needs or a business school's requirements.

Outward Bound operates from five residential centres in the Lake District, Wales and Scotland, each with dormitories accommodating about 100 people. Each of the sites is well placed for access to mountain and water activities and contains mountain huts, log cabins, and overnight camping sites. Comfortable quarters are used for indoor instruction and debriefings.

Outward Bound is well equipped with vehicles, boats, canoes, climbing equipment and camping gear which is made available to course participants.

Outward Bound has over 40 years' experience of providing personal development courses which complement academic and business training. Over the years the range of courses has been extended to meet the needs of all age groups and now offers a cost-effective training resource to commerce and industry.

The value of 'off-the-job-training' has long been recognised; but many classroom-based, residential courses are criticised because they are often unrealistic, and present no real rewards or penalties. In comparison, Outward Bound, in using the outdoors, makes a great impact on participants. The activities which demand both physical and mental effort, develop planning, decision-making, problem-solving, team work, leadership and communication skills and are followed by analysis and review sessions. Because these lessons are learned against the background of real projects and exercises, they are brought home with a vividness not achieved by classroom role-play sessions.

Participants gain a clear understanding of group dynamics, of their effect on others and of how others respond to them. They also gain a fresh insight into their own potential strengths and weaknesses and a new self-confidence borne out of increased achievement.

Outward Bound does not provide endurance training and individuals are not required to prove themselves – they are not assessed on their degree of fitness or skill in any of the activities, but rather on the effort and the contribution they make to the group. The lessons learned enhance academic, technical and commercial skills, and improve cooperation, communication and under-standing.

Outward Bound Wales has two centres close by each other on the north shore of the river Dovey and the coast of mid-Wales. They work closely together under one management and share some facilities.

Aberdovey. Situated one mile from the village, this was the first Outward Bound school and was opened in 1941. It can accommodate 120 students and offers a full range of outdoor training although there is a strong emphasis on water-based activities.

Rhowniar. Located half a mile away from the sea with accommodation for 80 students, the centre lies in an estate comprising of woods, meadows and large gardens. In addition to all the outdoor activities, a well-equipped drama hall facilitates indoor creative workshop sessions.

Outward Bound is also based in the Lake District, at *Eskdale* in a fine mansion set in wooded grounds with its own small lake, in one of the least frequented valleys of the Lake District, reaching from the coast at Ravenglass to the wold and magnificent mountain landscape below Scafell Pike. The centre accommodates 120 and offers the full range of courses with particular emphasis on mountain-based activities. A large detached house nearby can be used as a separate centre for 24 people on adult management courses or for those requiring more privacy.

Ullswater. Situated near Penrith, with excellent rail and

road communications, this 17th century house accommodates 90 students and is set in extensive grounds on the
west shore of the lake. There are views of mountain ranges
to the south dominated by Helvellyn. Lying in the heart of
countryside ideally suited to outdoor activities where
tracks and buildings are sparse, the school offers a wide
variety of activities, including all-year-round skiing and a
well-equipped lecture theatre for indoor sessions.

In Scotland, Outward Bound is based in *Loch Eil*. Situated
on the edge of a sea loch near Fort William, the centre
accommodates 90 and offers students a variety of Outward Bound courses as well as skill training in mountain
and sailing craft. One thousand square miles of mountains, islands, rivers, sea lochs, forest and wilderness
between the Grampian mountains and Hebridean islands
provide the terrain for a wide range of water and
mountain-based activities.

OML Associates

Willowbrook
Yarley Hill
Wells
Somerset BA5 1PA
(0749) 76103

The orientation of OML is in management and organisational development. Toward this end they use many
approaches including outdoor development. They work
with first line managers to directors, the average age of
their participants being 40. OML's outdoor management
development course has three main purposes:

1   to help managers to develop their style and system of
    managing in response to major changes in the nature
    of their jobs or organisations;
2   to develop managerial leadership skills to improve
    the effectiveness of teams operating under deman-
    ding conditions;

3 to provide experienced managers with an objective and rigorous test of their overall managerial skills under a variety of conditions of uncertainty and stress.

The specific aims of the outdoor management development course are:

1 to help experienced managers to extend their skills and managerial style to cope with change;
2 to test and develop skills of team working, leadership, and organisation, in a range of different managerial situations of increasing uncertainty;
3 to increase self-awareness, and to develop a better understanding of human behaviour;
4 to develop a broader and more considered approach to managerial problems and planning.

OML also offers tailor-made outdoor development programmes to meet an organisation's special needs.

OML does not have its own outdoor site but rather uses the facilities of Outward Bound Trust in various locations.

The chief trainers of OML tested the course design they now use with 20 outdoor development programmes run for the Imperial Group.

The River Dart Residential Centre

Holne Park
Ashburton
Newton Abbot
Devon TQ13 7NP
Ashburton (0364) 52511

The River Dart Residential Centre is owned by the River Dart Country Park Ltd. The centre is situated in a country mansion in 80 acres of parkland and gardens on the south-eastern edge of Dartmoor, one mile from Ashburton, 200 feet above sea level. The River Dart itself forms the mile-long eastern boundary of the centre. The grounds include lakes and woods for outdoor activities.

Dartmoor provides excellent walking and climbing areas. The River Dart is fine for canoeing and there are local limestone caves at Buckfastleigh.

The centre designs programmes for young people to develop leadership potential and team-building skills on trainee development courses. But they also run courses in leadership where the objectives are stated as enabling the participants to:

1 explore and experiment with different leadership styles;
2 attain a clear understanding of the processes at work when people interact in groups;
3 become more aware of the effect of their own behaviour on others;
4 develop their personal skills in group situations;
5 develop team-building and decision-making skills;
6 develop personal potential and increase self-confidence.

This residential course starts at midday on Monday and runs till breakfast on Saturday.

The staff at the centre also help companies with their own in-company programmes and their involvement can take various forms:

1 they run standard courses entirely for the client's staff;
2 they design specific courses to meet the needs of differing organisations, tailored where necessary to include specialist speakers;
3 they run courses jointly with in-company trainers;
4 they run joint union/management courses in a neutral environment.

The Sail Training Association (STA)

2a The Hard
Portsmouth PO1 3PT
(0705) 832055

The STA is a registered charity that conducts sail training races and operates a training programme for young men and women between the ages of 16 and 24 aboard schooners. The STA runs the programme on two-week voyages in its two 300-ton topsail schooners, the *Sir Winston Churchill* and the *Malcolm Miller*.

The scheme was originally started as a philanthropic endeavour to give young people a character-building experience. But it has earned a place in the industrial training field and is in part funded by company training budgets as well as charity. Since 1970 all cruise fees have been subsidised by the STA by about 25 per cent.

The programme itself consists of putting 39 young people on a large sailing ship under expert guidance to sail a course of 800–1000 miles of ocean.

The voyage puts the young people in an entirely unfamiliar environment facing them with an open ocean and a complex system of ropes, spars and sails. It also provides a spirit of adventure which elicits enthusiasm and cooperation. In this atmosphere the need for both personal and group discipline emerges. Without an acceptance of discipline the voyage would grind to a halt and lives would be endangered. Finally, like all outdoor development programmes the voyage extends the individuals involved requiring them to break through physical and psychological barriers.

To attract sponsors and demonstrate the impact of the youth training programme STA runs a limited number of one-week cruises each year for adults only. Industrialists who want to 'get away from it all' are welcome on these cruises.

Trainees need no previous experience of the sea or of sailing; neither do they have to be in A1 physical condition. Trainee crews have included handicapped persons – deaf, epileptic, diabetic, with artificial limbs, etc. Special safety precautions are taken for non-swimmers.

The STA's patron is the Duke of Edinburgh.

Sea Training and Development

118 Wellesley Road
Ilford IG1 4LD
(01) 518 0373

The organisation designs courses to meet their client's developmental needs particularly focusing on senior managers and management teams.

The tailor-made courses look at learning, coaching, appraisal and leadership skills and these processes are related to ideas about trust and teams.

The activities take place aboard a comfortably appointed, large cruising yacht. Programmes are normally six days, but could be longer.

Simulon

16 Millfields Avenue
Hillmorton
Rugby
Rugby 4821

Simulon provides only custom designed programmes. They are designed to focus on
1   individual development, self-understanding, confidence building;
2   social skills, group dynamics, relating to and working with others;
3   understanding organisations and societies of people.

A typical programme is six days but Simulon does also run three-day and 14-day programmes. The organisation claims to make 'use of the outdoors from a background of training and development experience, and not the other way round'.

Clients include:

Plessey
Rio Tinto Zinc
Portals Holdings
Marconi

Travellers

Waterside
Kendal
Cumbria LA9 4HE
(0539) 28334

Travellers is a noted consultancy that arranges a wide programme of outdoor education, travel and adventure programmes for various agencies, societies, and management.

'Leadership is the lifting of vision to higher sights, the raising of performance to a higher standard.' This rather exalted definition of leadership fits nicely into the primary work of Travellers – organising expeditions or wilderness journeys. The members of Travellers team have specialist knowledge of the remote cultures and regions where they conduct their outdoor activities. These include the Himalayan region with a range of 15–38-day treks. Trips to the Alps, Norway and Arctic wilderness are also offered with 7–14-day treks available; East African expeditions for 16 days.

The outdoor programme can be designed to meet the particular client's requirements whether they are senior managers or a national sporting body.

YMCA National Centre

Lakeside
Ulverston
Cumbria LA12 8BD
Newby Bridge (0448) 31758

The YMCA has been directly involved with development training for young people in industry since it began in London in 1844. Today it continues to play an important role with the Manpower Services Commission (MSC) such as in the YMCA-organised training for life scheme. The YMCA National Centre at Lakeside helped design the model for Youth Opportunity Programme (YOP), the forerunner to the present Youth Training Scheme (YTS).

The Lakeside Centre is located on the south-western shores of Windermere, in the Lake District National Park. For more than 25 years, this centre has designed and pioneered development training courses for the specific needs of industry. Helping make young people responsible 'industrious citizens' is their goal.

Their range of courses for young people includes induction courses and personal development courses. They also run special training courses working closely with industrial training boards and colleges to provide residential courses for young workers, both skilled and unskilled, and for the unemployed. There is also a youth at work service and open industrial courses.

Under the banner of leadership development, the Centre offers two programmes.

For supervisors. Those in positions of responsibility are given the opportunity to assess their supervisory capabilities and to develop further the skills necessary to manage more effectively. Emphasis is placed on good leadership by examining leadership styles and roles in a variety of practical situations. Opportunities are available for individuals to develop their communication skills, to learn to coordinate problem-solving activities and to come to terms with demanding hours and working under pressure. Regular review discussions ensure that learning can be effectively transferred back to the work situation. Programme inputs include initiative problems, team-work exercises, creative project work and expeditions, as well as outdoor activities.

For managers. For those with staff management responsibilities, who wish to sharpen their management skills and the ability to obtain results through other people, emphasis is placed on the balancing of task achievement with group and personal achievement. Candidates are presented with real situations, requiring commitment, judgement and genuine decision making under pressure. The ability to use a variety of leadership styles, assess priorities and make firm decisions is highlighted. Formal input sessions and discussions are complemented by a progressive outdoor programme involving group problem-solving situations and challenge. A stimulating break from work is provided, together with the opportunity to re-evaluate personal attitudes.

The YMCA's client list for its Lakeside Centre includes a half dozen national training boards plus a wide assortment of companies, including:

Alcan (Lynemouth) Ltd
Allbright and Wilson Ltd
Central Electricity Generating Board
Civil Aviation Authority
Corning Ltd
General Electricity Company Telecommunications Ltd
Greater Manchester Police
IMA Yorkshire Imperial
Imperial Chemical Industries PLC
Kirkstall Forge Engineering Ltd
Metal Box Co Ltd
Merseyside Fire Services
NEI Parsons Ltd
NEI Reyrolle Ltd
NSK Bearings Europe Ltd
Otis Elevators Co Ltd
Paper and Paper Product Industry Training Board
Rubber and Plastics Processing Industry Training Board
Shell UK Oil
Thermal Syndicate Ltd
Thorn Heating Ltd

UK Fertilizers Ltd
Vickers Shipbuilding and Engineering Ltd
Warwickshire Constabulary Cadet Training Dept.

RELEVANT ASSOCIATIONS

These two interlinked organisations are helpful for outdoor development:

National Advice and Information Centre

DMIHE
High Melton
Doncaster
Tel: Mexborough (0709) 582 427

Begun in 1981 by the National Association for Outdoor Education and the Doncaster Metropolitan Institute of Higher Education, the National Advice and Information Centre is founded by the Jubilee Trust. The centre has piloted courses on special school children and young adult offenders.

National Association for Outdoor Education (NAOE)

The Director
National Advice and Information Centre
DMIHE
High Melton
Doncaster
Tel: Mexborough (0709) 582 427

The National Association for Outdoor Education (NAOE) was inaugurated in 1970 before the boom in outdoor education. As growth continues, the role of the association in providing advice, information and support has become more important.

The aims of NAOE are:

1   to ensure that outdoor education is of a standard compatible with the needs and abilities of young people;
2   to identify, examine and report upon problems within outdoor education;
3   to ensure an efficient information and publicity service;
4   to further the recognition of outdoor education as an integral part of the educational system within the United Kingdom.

The official journal of NAOE is *The Journal of Adventure Education*.

APPENDIX

The documents reproduced in this Appendix form part of the material designed for the research project described in Part II of the book. The two tables are included here for the benefit of other researchers who may wish to pursue some of the opportunities they indicate.

CRANFIELD SCHOOL OF MANAGEMENT

RESEARCH: OUTDOOR DEVELOPMENT – TIME OFF WORK OR A RELEVANT TRAINING METHOD?

RESPONDENT COMPANIES WHO USE OUTDOOR DEVELOPMENT

Title of organisation	Additional comments/ material?	Prepared to discuss further?
A.M.I.	Y	Y
N.G. BAILEY	Y	Y
BEJAMS	N	Y
BENTALLS	Y	Y
BERGER	N	Y
BRITISH HOME STORES	N	Y
COATES PATONS	N	Y
DE LA RUE	N	N
DRG TRAINING COLLEGE	Y	Y
ELANCO	N	Y
FOSTER MENSWEAR	N	N
GALLIFORD BRINDLEY	N	Y
GEC	Y	Y
GKN	Y	Y
HADEN PLC	Y	Y
HARGREAVES	N	Y
KODAK	N	Y
LAVEZEE	Y	Y
MARTINS NEWSAGENTS	Y	Y
MMB	N	Y
NESTLE	N	Y
NORTHERN FOODS	Y	Y
PILKINGTONS	Y	Y
PLESSEY (10W)	N	N
PLESSEY LIVERPOOL	Y	Y
PORTALS	N	Y/N (2 Resps)
RHM	N	Y
ROUSSEL LABS.	Y	Y
ROWNTREE MACKINTOSH	N	Y

RTZ	Y	Y
SAINSBURY	N	Y
SALVESEN	N	Y
SECURICOR	Y	Y
SILENTNIGHT	Y	Y
T. SILVEY	Y	N
SOUND ATTENUATORS LIMITED	Y	Y
TECALAMIT	Y	Y
TERRAIN	Y	Y
TESCO	Y	N
WEIR PUMPS	Y	N
UNION INTERNATIONAL	Y	N
G. WIMPEY	N	Y
WRIGLEY	Y	Y
LEX SERVICE PLC	Y	Y
LITTLEWOODS ORGANISATION PLC	Y	N
LONDON BRICK PRODUCTS LTD	Y	Y
LOW & BONAR PLC	Y	Y
LRC PRODUCTS LTD	Y	Y
LUNCHEON VOUCHERS LTD	N	N
MACMILLAN PUBLISHERS LTD	Y	Y
MASSEY FERGUSON LTD	Y	Y
MARSHALL OF CAMBRIDGE LTD	Y	N
MCKECHNIE BROTHERS PLC	N	N
MIDSHIRES BUILDING SOCIETY	Y	N
MK ELECTRIC LTD	N	N
MOLINS PLC	N	N
NSS NEWSAGENTS RETAIL LTD	N	N
ODHAMS-SUN PRINTERS LTD	N	Y
OFFREX GROUP PLC	Y	N
PFIZER LTD	Y	Y
PHILLIPS ELECTRONICS	N	Y
POWELL DUFFRYN PLC	Y	Y
RCA LTD	Y	N
READERS DIGEST ASSOC. LTD	N	N
READICUT INTERNATIONAL PLC	Y	N
ROCHE PRODUCTS LTD	N	Y
RUSTON BUCYRUS LTD	N	N
SANDELL PERKINS PLC	N	Y
SANDOZ PRODUCTS LTD	N	N
G.D. SEARLE & CO LTD	N	Y
SMITH KLINE FRENCH LABS LTD	N	N
STAVELEY INDUSTRIES PLC	N	N
STEETLEY PLC	Y	N

TENNECO EUROPE LTD	Y	N
TRICENTROL OIL CORP. LTD.	N	Y
UNION CARBIDE UK LTD	Y	Y
VAUXHALL MOTORS LTD	N	Y
VICKERS PLC	N	Y
J. WADDINGTON PLC	N	N
WARD WHITE & NEWALL PLC	Y	N
WATSON & PHILIP PLC	Y	N
WEETABIX LTD	Y	Y
J. WEDGWOOD & SONS LTD	Y	N
THE 600 GROUP PLC	Y	N

ANALYSIS OF NON-CURRENT USERS

This section looks at the immediate response of the non-current users. The non-current users are split out horizontally by the reason given for non-use (see questionnaire) and split out vertically as those who responded 'yes' to the various questions.

	Cost–benefit ratio too high	Considered and found irrelevant	Never considered	Other	Total
Total no. in category	9	20	39	24	92
Have you ever used outdoor development activities?	5 55%	2 10%	4 10%	10 42%	21 23%
Prepared to discuss OD with Cranfield	4 44%	9 45%	16 41%	15 63%	44 47%
Would you like to receive a summary of research?	4 44%	15 75%	28 72%	20 83%	67 73%
Was any comment made by respondent?	5 55%	6 30%	18 45%	12 50%	41 45%

There is a high level of interest here, in spite of the fact that the majority or respondents have never actually used outdoor development. The majority are prepared to discuss the subject and are interested in the research conclusions.

OUTDOOR DEVELOPMENT RESEARCH PROJECT
CRANFIELD SCHOOL OF MANAGEMENT

FORM A   CURRENT USER OF OUTDOOR DEVELOPMENT PROGRAMMES

1) COMPANY NAME:

2) ADDRESS:

3) TELEPHONE:

4) PERSONNEL DIRECTOR/MANAGER:

5) PERSON RESPONSIBLE FOR OUTDOOR DEVELOPMENT:

6) DATE OUTDOOR DEVELOPMENT FIRST USED:

7) WHERE DID YOUR COMPANY FIRST HEAR OF OUTDOOR DEVELOPMENT?

Journal/magazine/newspaper ☐   From educational establishments ☐
Seminar on management development ☐   From outdoor development organisations ☐
Television/radio ☐   From government agencies ☐
From other companies ☐   From consultants ☐
From professional bodies ☐

8) NO. OF COMPANY PARTICIPANTS PER YEAR (APPROX):

9) LEVEL OF RESPONSIBILITY OF PARTICIPANTS:

10) PLEASE RANK THE BENEFITS GAINED AS TO THEIR IMPORTANCE
    a) Personal development ( )
    b) Team development ( )
    c) Leadership development ( )
    d) Communication workshop ( )
    e) Managing in uncertainty ( )
    f) Other (please specify):

11) ORGANISATION USED:
    a) In-house:
    b) Brathay Hall Trust:
    c) Challenge Training:
    d) Leadership Trust
    e) Outward Bound:
    f) Other (please specify):

12) PRINCIPAL ACTIVITY/ACTIVITIES USED:

13) DO YOU FORMALLY EVALUATE OUTDOOR DEVELOPMENT PROGRAMMES?   YES □   NO □

14) ARE YOU PREPARED TO DISCUSS THE USE OF OUTDOOR DEVELOPMENT WITH A REPRESENTATIVE OF CRANFIELD
    SCHOOL OF MANAGEMENT?   YES □   NO □

15) DOES A TRAINER FROM YOUR COMPANY ACCOMPANY OUTDOOR COURSES?
    NEVER □   SOMETIMES □   FREQUENTLY □   ALWAYS □

16) HAVE THERE BEEN ANY SERIOUS ACCIDENTS DURING YOUR OUTDOOR DEVELOPMENT COURSES?   YES □   NO □
    (if yes, please specify number and nature of accident)

PLEASE ADD OVERLEAF ANY FURTHER COMMENTS. HOW DO YOU SEE THE FUTURE GROWTH OF OUTDOOR DEVELOPMENT?

DATE:_____   SIGNED:_____

I WOULD LIKE TO RECEIVE A SUMMARY OF THE RESEARCH CONCLUSIONS   YES □   NO □

167

OUTDOOR DEVELOPMENT RESEARCH PROJECT
CRANFIELD SCHOOL OF MANAGEMENT

FORM B   NON-CURRENT USER OF OUTDOOR DEVELOPMENT PROGRAMMES

1) COMPANY NAME: _____

2) ADDRESS: _____

3) TELEPHONE: _____

4) PERSONNEL DIRECTOR/MANAGER: _____

5) TRAINING MANAGER: _____

6) HAVE YOU EVER USED OUTDOOR DEVELOPMENT ACTIVITIES?   YES ☐   NO ☐

7) WE DO **NOT** USE OUTDOOR DEVELOPMENT BECAUSE.....

     a) Cost–benefit ratio is too high: ( )

     b) We have considered it and found it is   ( )
        irrelevant to our needs:

     c) We have not considered it: ( )

     d) Other (please specify):   ( )

8) WE MIGHT CONSIDER USING OUTDOOR DEVELOPMENT PROGRAMMES FOR THE FOLLOWING REASONS.

9) PLEASE TICK HERE IF YOU WOULD BE PREPARED TO DISCUSS THE USE OF OUTDOOR DEVELOPMENT PROGRAMMES WITH A REPRESENTATIVE OF CRANFIELD SCHOOL OF MANAGEMENT.

YES ☐   NO ☐

DATE: _____   SIGNATURE: _____

I WOULD LIKE TO RECEIVE A SUMMARY OF THE RESEARCH CONCLUSIONS

YES ☐   NO ☐

REFERENCES

1   Bonington, C. *Quest for Adventure*, Hodder and Stoughton, London, 1972, p 13.

2   Mortlock, C. J. *Adventure Education*, Keswick Ferguson, London, 1978.

3   Williams, D. H. 'Adventure with a Purpose', *The Training Officer*, October 1980.

4   Keeting, S. 'A Case Study in Outdoor Development: the Dangerous Sports Club Kilimanjaro Expedition', 6–21 January 1979. (MBA Paper available from J. A. Bank, Cranfield School of Management, Cranfield Bedfordshire), p 17.

5   Beeby, M. and Rathbourne, S. 'Development Training: Using the Outdoors for Management Development', *Association of Teachers of Management Journal*, Autumn 1983.

6   Wright, A. W. 'Participative Education and the Inevitable Revolution', *Journal of Creative Behaviour*, vol. 4, 1970.

7   Kolb, D. A., Rubin, M. I. and McIntyre, J. M. *Organizational Psychology – an Experiential Approach*, Prentice–Hall, Englewood Cliffs, N. J. 1971.

8   Waters, J. A. 'Managerial Skill Development', *Academy of Management Review*, vol. 5, No. 3, pp. 449-453.

9   Foy, N. *The Yin and Yang of Organisations*, Grant McIntyre, London 1981, pp. 217-218.

10   Ibid, p.222.

11   Revans, R. W. *Action Learning: New Techniques for Management*, Blond and Briggs, London, 1980, p 288.

12   EFMD – European Foundation for Management Development, *Management Education in the European Community*, Brussels and Luxemburg: Office for Official Publications of the European Community, 1978, p.38.

13   Revans, R. W. op. cit. (note 11), p.288.

14   Perhaps the most active advocate of action-centred leadership is: The Industrial Society, Peter Runge House, 3 Carlton House Terrace, London SW1Y 5DG Tel: 01 839 4300.

15   Adair, J. *Action-centred Leadership*, Gower, Aldershot 1982.

16   Personal interview.

17   Creswick, C. and Williams, R. *Using the Outdoors for*

Management Development and Team Building, The Food, Drink and Tobacco Industry Training Board, Gloucester, 1979, p.3.

18 Hawrylyshyn, B. 'Preparing Managers for International Operations', *The Business Quarterly,* Autumn 1967, p.31.

19 Ibid.

20 Creswick, C. and Williams, op. cit., p.3.

21 Ibid.

22 Personal interview. See Bonington, C. *Everest the Hard Way: The First Ascent of the South West Face,* Hodder and Stoughton. 1976.

23 Kidder, T. *The Soul of a New Machine,* Penguin, London, 1983, p.12.

24 For the history of Outward Bound see: Wilson, R. *Inside Outward Bound,* McIntyre, Vancouver, 1981; James, D., (Ed.), *Outward Bound,* Routledge and Kegan Paul, London, 1958.

25 The Center For Creative Leadership, Greensborough, North Carolina, USA.

26 'Curriculum 11–16', Working Paper by H. M. Inspectorate, 'A Contribution to the Current Debate'.

27 'Learning out of Doors', An HMI Survey of outdoor education and short-stay residential experience, issued by the Department of Education and Science, p.47.

28 Beer, M. 'Technology of Organisational Development', in Dunnette, *Handbook of Industrial and Organisational Psychology,* Rand McNally College Publishing Co., Chicago, p.956.

29 Toffler, A. *The Third Wave*, William Collins, London, 1980.

30 Schein, E. H. *Organizational Psychology*, Prentice-Hall, Englewood Cliffs, N.J. 1965.

31 Beer, M. op. cit. (note 28)

32 Levinson, D.J. 'Role, Personality and Social Structure', *Journal of Abnormal and Social Psychology*, Vol. 58, 1959, pp.170-80.

33 Pugh, D. 'Role Activation Conflict: A Study of Industrial Inspection', *American Sociology Review*, Vol. 31, No. 6, 1966, p.836.

34 Blake, R. R. and Mouton, J. S. *Building a Dynamic Corporation through Grid Organisation Development Reading*, Addison-Wesley, Mass. 1969.

35 Radcliff, P. and Keslake, P. 'Outward Bound?' in Boydell, T. and Peddler, M. (Eds) *Management Self-Development, Concepts and Practices*, Gower, Aldershot, 1981, p.88.

36 Thoreau, H. D. *What I lived for, Walden*, vol 2, AMS Publishers, New York, 1981.

37 Levinson, H. 'When Executives Burn Out', *Harvard Business Review*, May–June 1981, pp. 73–81.

38 Maslach, C. *Burnout. The Cost of Caring*, Prentice-Hall, Englewood Cliffs, N. J., 1982, p.3. See also Maslach, C. and Jackson, S. E. *M.B.I: Maslach Burnout Inventory*, Consulting Psychologists Press, Palo Alto, Ca., 1981.

39 Freudenberger, H. J. *Burn-out: The Melancholy of High Achievement*, Doubleday, New York, 1980, p.17.

40 Cherniss, C. *Staff Burnout, Job Stress in the Human Services,* Sage Publications, Beverly Hills, Ca. 1980, p.18. See also Cherniss, C. *Professional Burnout in Human Service Organizations,* Praeger Publishers, 1980.

41 Veninga, R. L. and Spradley, J. P. *The Work-Stress Connection: How to cope with Job Burnout,* Little, Brown and Co., Boston, 1981, p.6.

42 Levinson, op. cit. (note 37), p.77.

43 Ginsberg as referred to in an unpublished paper on Burn-out by A. Garden (MIT, Boston).

44 Tubesings, D. A. *Kicking Your Stress Habits,* Signet Books, New American Library, New York. N.A.L.

45 Potter, B.A. *Beating Job Burnout,* Harbor Publications, San Francisco, 1980.

46 Freudenberger op. cit. (note 39), p. 13.

47 Ouchi, W. *Theory Z: How American Business Can Meet the Japanese Challenge,* Addison-Wesley, Reading, Maryland, 1981.

48 Peters, T. J. and Waterman, R. H. 'In Search of Excellence', *Lessons from America's Best Run Companies,* New York, 1982.

49 Ibid., pp. 80 and 323.

50 Radcliff, P. and Keslake, P. op. cit. (note 35), p. 88

51 Peters, T. J. and Waterman, R. H. op. cit. (note 48).

52 Ibid.

53 Ibid.

54   Gilbert-Smith, D. 'The Leadership Trust', brochure, 1983, p.3.

55   Adair, J. op. cit. (note 15).

56   Brochures and course descriptions are available from: Colorado Outward Bound School, 945 Pennsylvania, Denver, Colorado, 80203, USA.

57   Toffler, A. op. cit. (note 29).

58   Mansell, C. 'How GEC Learns Action', *Management Today*, May 1975, p. 64.

59   From a talk to the conference 'The Growing Use of the Outdoors', sponsored by the British Institute of Management, London, 14 June 1983.

60   'I thought we were having a film show', TV South documentary by Peter Williams. First broadcast on 17 February 1983 to TV South area and later broadcast nationwide. See also 'The Money Programme', BBC 2 24 October 1982, for Henley Management Course at Outward Bound.

61   King, P. and Harmon, P. *Evaluation of the Colorado Outward Bound School's Career Development Course Offered in Collaboration with the Training Education and Employee Development Department of Martin-Marietta Aerospace*, Harmon Associates, San Francisco, 1981, pp.4–5.

62   Isenhart, M. W. 'An Investigation of the Interface Between Corporate Leadership Needs and the Outward Bound Experience', published by and available from the Colorado Outward Bound School.

63   Personal communications.

64   Rose, Charles, *MBA Report*, Cranfield School of Management.

65 Personal communication.

66 King, op, cit. (note 61).

67 Steinem, G. *Outrageous Acts and Everyday Rebellions,* Jonathan Cape, London, 1984, p. 200.

68 *Sex Discrimination, A Guide to the Sex Discrimination Act 1975,* Home Office, HMSO, London, 1975, pp. 34-36.

69 Personal communication.

70 Mager, R. F. *Preparing Objectives for Programmed Instructions,* Fearon Publishers, San Francisco, 1962.

71 Elliot, C. K. and Knibbs, 'European Training', 1982.

72 Elliott, C. K. (work in progress).

73 Mossman, A. 'Management Development Using the Outdoors: Action and Reflection to Help Managers Face the Challenges Confronting them at Work'. A report to the LGTB, 1982.

74 Hesseling, P. *Strategy of Evaluation Research,* Van Gorcum and Company, Netherlands 1966, p. 302.

75 Roberts K., White, G.E. and Parker, H.J. *The Charac-ter-training Industry, Adventure-training Schemes in Britain,* David and Charles, Newton Abbot, 1974, pp. 148-166.

76 Allison, G. T. *Essence of Decision: Explaining the Cuban Missile Crisis,* Little, Brown and Co., Boston, 1971.

77 Mintzberg, H. 'The Manager's Job: Folklore and Fact', *Harvard Business Review,* July–August 1975, p. 60.

78 Drucker, P. F. *Managing in Turbulent Times,*

Heinemann, London, 1980, pp. 219-24; *The Practice of Management,* Heinemann, London, 1968, p. 13.

79   From a talk to the conference 'The Growing Use of the Outdoors', op. cit. (note 59).

80   Cole, J. 'Combining Learning and Assessment: A Unique Approach to Developing Young Managers', *Training Officer,* March 1983, p. 69.

81   Ibid. p. 71

82   From a talk to the conference, 'The Growing Use of the Outdoors', op. cit. (note 59).

83   Ibid.